OWN YOUR
PURPOSE

JEREMY SCOTT ASKINS

TRILOGY
A WHOLLY OWNED SUBSIDIARY OF TBN
PROFESSIONAL PUBLISHING MEETS POWERFUL PROMOTION

FOREWORD

If you have bought this book and made it to this page, I know you are searching and hungry to either find or grow and move in your purpose. If you continue reading this book, Jeremy Askins is going to take you on a journey on how to own your purpose in a way that you have never heard before. His vulnerability in the following pages will draw you in to examining yourself, and if you let it, once you acknowledge the things that are brought out, this book will transform your life!

I have known Jeremy for many years, first as a cousin, then as a friend, then as a husband and father to his wife and kids, then as a phenomenal leader in our church. I've known for a long time that he has had more to offer than he has even realized. I genuinely believe this book is just the beginning for what God wants to do in using him to help others through his experiences. I have seen Jeremy in good times. I have seen Jeremy in bad times. I have seen Jeremy healed. I have seen Jeremy broken. I have seen Jeremy laugh. I have seen Jeremy cry. During every season I have seen him, he is always open to what God has for him and how he can learn and grow and share his story with anyone he can to help them experience the God he has experienced.

You can expect this book to be challenging and very motivating. You can expect to feel joy, sadness, anger, frustration, and love. But whenever God reveals those things, He intends to heal those areas in your life revealed that need His grace and love. I pray this book will uncover some areas of your life that you haven't looked at in a long time, or maybe ever, and in that process of seeing all these things, you will find your healing to move forward in your purpose.

Whether you are down and out right now or on a mountaintop, there is still more out there for you. There's still more purpose for you. I promise that as you read through the following pages and chapters, you will be inspired to dig deeper with God and find new ways to obey as the Holy Spirit directs you.

You have a purpose! Now it's time to activate it and learn how to walk in what God has called you to do. If you feel like quitting and giving up, you are reading the right book. I hope that as Jeremy shares his stories and struggles, the Holy Spirit meets you right where you're at. Your life is about to change forever! Don't give up now!

Go into the rest of this book with your heart open to whatever God wants to do inside of you so you can learn to Own Your Purpose - Through Obedience.

Jeremy Kriegbaum

Pastor - Mercy Point Church

ACKNOWLEDGEMENTS

I would like to thank my wife Stephanie for partnering with me on this journey of life. Thank you for making our house a home. I love what we have become together. Thank you for getting me to open my eyes and see the love of God in our lives that I had once abandoned.

Thank you to our five beautiful children. What a true blessing they are. To Jonah, Noah, Delilah, Micah, and Elliana: you make Dad proud each and every day. I can't wait to see your purpose being fulfilled in this life.

To my parents Rebecca and Edward, thank you for the encouragement and strength to get to it. You helped me be brave enough to chase life and the pursuit of all it offers.

Thank you to my Uncle Warren and Aunt Tammy for always seeing that my life had a bigger purpose than I was living.

Thank you to our church leadership team for doing nothing but speaking life into me during this process. Pastors Jeremy and Janelle, thank you for taking a chance on me. I'm so thankful for all the love over the years, even though I didn't deserve it, and seeing that God had plans for me all along.

There are so many people I could also mention, but the list would go on forever. Know that I appreciate all those that have given me encouragement.

Thank You, Jesus, for mending my broken pieces, breathing new life into me, saving me from myself, and giving me the purpose to write this book to share with everyone.

LET'S BEGIN.

I

ON PURPOSE

We are all born into this world unique. Unique locations, different times, different parents, family situations, etc. Some of us are born into the appealingly perfect family-mom, dad, two kids (one boy, one girl), a family dog, maybe a cat or some other type of pet. They live on a perfect street with no crime, no traffic, great neighbors from whom to borrow a bowl of sugar (if people still do that) from time to time, ideal lawn with a perfectly painted stain-free white picket fence, a driveway with no bumps or rocks, perfectly paved and maintained yearly. An inviting sidewalk leads to a perfect front door of an ideal house that is perfectly painted and says "Come on in" as you stand on the perfectly maintained sisal door mat that screams WELCOME. You know this kind of mat.

Then, most of us are born into some uncertainty, disorganized chaos, and not-quite-perfect situations that

11

are challenging or welcoming, depending on what is influencing them. You don't have everything you ever wanted; you don't quite get it; you have to strive to find your place in all you do.

No one has the same story, upbringing, or environment. Everyone has a story that is theirs. However, one thing that we all have in common is we are all born with a purpose that is perfectly designed for us, a purpose that can only be fulfilled as it is designed for you by God.

We are all put on this Earth at a predetermined time and place, into a specific family; because you are here on purpose and you are needed for a time such as this. It is incredible that God placed us in a designated place and time, knowing that you are planned to fulfill the purpose you are called to. Even thousands of years ago, God had your purpose set for you at this specific time of your life. Accepting this is hard, because we assign our time and limits to this thought. How can this be? How can we be significant enough to have an assigned purpose for a long time before we were born? In Luke 12:7 , Jesus goes on to say, "Indeed, the very hairs on your head are numbered. Do not fear, you are more valuable than many sparrows."

IF YOU ARE IMPORTANT ENOUGH FOR GOD TO KNOW EXACTLY THE COUNT OF HAIRS ON YOUR HEAD, HE HAS A PURPOSE AND A PLAN FOR YOUR LIFE.

What is purpose? It is defined as this:

The reason for which something is done or created or for which something exists. You exist to fulfill your purpose, to own your purpose that God has given you. You are here to satisfy the reason, the purpose, you are here. You are here at this specific time for God's specific reason. Your being here is for something that will be up to you to fulfill. No one can do what you are called to do like you can. It will get done as God sees it even if you don't step into your purpose. However, it will just not be to the full extent of what it was intended. We will talk about David and Saul later in the book.

Throughout this book, we are going to touch on many aspects of purpose, taking a journey through the Bible to give you a better overall understanding of what God has for you. Backing up the thoughts here biblically will not only help you understand your calling but also teach you how to hear from God and how to eliminate obstacles that are frustrating and distractions that hold you back from owning your purpose.

WHO ARE YOU?

_____

_____

_____

_____

WHAT DO YOU LIKE/DISLIKE ABOUT YOURSELF?

_____

_____

_____

_____

HOW DO YOU DEFINE YOUR PURPOSE? DO YOU KNOW WHAT IT IS?

_____

_____

_____

_____

HOW DO YOU PURSUE YOUR PURPOSE? WHAT DO I NEED TO DO TO FULFILL IT?

_____

_____

_____

_____

WHAT IF I'M NOT IN MY PURPOSE? HOW DO I GET ON TRACK?

_____

_____

_____

_____

WHAT IF I FEEL I'M NOT GOOD ENOUGH?

_____

_____

_____

_____

God never assigns someone a purpose that they are not equipped to fulfill. It does not mean that purpose is easy and pain-free. Often, the purpose is challenging, confusing, and not always understood, and many times it will take you out of your comfort zone to stretch you into what you are capable of achieving or being. When you are walking in your purpose, you will face storms and obstacles; they will challenge you and make it hard for you to move forward. You can feel like you are climbing a never-ending mountain or face a storm that you feel like you are not going to make it through rather than move forward without opposition. Everyone likes the easy path. This is why highways or flying are the preferred way to travel. Usually, little stops, obstacles, or opposition get in your way. We see here in Matthew what it's like to follow directions given by Jesus.

Matthew 14:22-25 says, "Immediately He made the disciples get into the boat and go ahead of Him to the other side, while He sent the crowds away. After He had sent the crowds away, He went up on the mountain by Himself to pray; when it was evening, He was there alone. But the boat was already a long distance from the land, battered by the waves, for the wind was contrary. And in the fourth watch of the night He came to them, walking on the sea."

They got in the boat as directed and were tossed around by the waves, struggling to reach their destination. Their momentary purpose was to follow what Jesus asked them to do, and it would have been so easy for them to turn around. I'm only assuming here, but there was probably a lot of conversation going on about what to do. Do we go back? Are we going to die? Then suddenly before dawn, still in their assignment to go to the other side of the lake, Jesus shows up doing the impossible: walking on the water. When we walk in our purpose, Jesus will always show up and show off in our life when needed, just when we think that we are not going to make it, not going to be good enough or have enough to make it happen. In Matthew 14:28, Peter steps out of the boat to walk to Jesus but makes one mistake. He begins to lose his focus on Jesus and gets distracted and frightened by the obstacles around him. He let the wind and waves become bigger than the Man that is walking on the water. The faith he had to step out of the boat and to walk on the water toward Jesus also began to waiver. As he started to sink, Jesus reached out and grabbed his hand, called him out for having little faith, and got him into the boat. It's easy to say, "Oh Peter, ye of little faith" as we read this story, but if you're being honest with yourself, we do this in our lives daily. We are constantly taking our eyes off Jesus when we need Him the most. If we can keep focused on God, our purpose will be so much easier to fulfill with God's help rather than us trying to do it ourselves.

God knows what He is doing and already knows what you will do, but it is still your choice to own your purpose and live the best life God has for you. Life is full of choices, and each one you make will have a consequence, good or bad, moving you forward or keeping you stagnant, not going in the direction you are called to go.

Your purpose is designed for you specifically, a perfect fit for you. It is not to be compared to others' purposes and it's not any less important than someone else's assignment. When you compare your purpose to another, it devalues what you're given, and that is counterproductive to your purpose. God never gives us more than we can process and fulfill when we include Him. We will face challenges, and it will not be easy. Fulfilling your purpose will not be easy because it wouldn't take God to lead you into it and through it, if it was.

Defining your purpose may be easy, or it may be confusing, but it won't always be clear to everyone around you. Other people might not understand or get your purpose, but find comfort in that it's yours, not theirs. I heard someone once say that the graveyard is the richest collection of treasure ever. It's full of people that are no longer here and never got to fulfill their calling or purpose. Maybe they didn't create the invention that was their purpose. Maybe because they were afraid or had insecurities about not being enough, the business they knew they should have started but never did—the church or school they were supposed to work at or attend.

> *"'For I know the plans I have for you,' declares the LORD, 'plans to prosper you and not to harm you, plans to give you hope and a future.'"*
>
> **Jeremiah 29:11**

God outlined and planned your life before you even made an appearance here on Earth. Have you taken the steps to live a life designed by God, to fulfill your purpose and live a life of faith and trust in God, to live a life of hope and life everlasting? It sounds like a lot, and it won't be easy to always trust God with all you do and to be under God's grand plan for your life.

Walking in your purpose will feel uncomfortable and awkward at times, because only sometimes are you going to know what is next. You will sometimes be unsure how you ever got where you are and may even have to look back in awe and wonder to see what God has accomplished in you and through you. Looking back will open your eyes to what God has brought you through and what experiences you have to help someone else that may need it.

Many times in my life, I have tried to do what I want when I want it, and it always seems to backfire eventually. You can walk a certain way, take whatever paths you choose, and may even have success doing so, but it will only be the best life for you if you strive to live out your purpose. Your peace won't be as great as it should or could be if you don't trust and have faith that your God has you and will keep you, not wanting for anything.

Your purpose doesn't always come from skills you acquire, but can be within you, waiting to be exposed by what God made you to be. Camera film can only be revealed through exposure at the right time with the required chemicals and equipment. The wrong time will lead to a ruined film and not come out as intended. Much like your purpose timing, the correct information and the proper use of tools will unlock your purpose with just the right amount of exposure. Too much exposure too soon will only lead to your purpose not coming out as God designs it. God gives us the tools to use. We have the Bible, prayer, and worship that will all put us into a closer position and relationship with God when we apply them in our lives. Guidance from others around you can play a big part in understanding what you feel called to. Remember, not everyone may be helpful and can also hurt you if their vision is different from yours. You have to talk to people that will encourage you, not distract you from what you feel God is calling you to.

Apples and oranges both have a purpose. They can grow easier in their proper environment. Apples need cold winters and harsh environmental conditions to activate the seeds and plants to create perfect fruit. Apples need many cold or chilly hours to grow to their potential, to grow into the desired fruit they become when the conditions of their development are ideal. Oranges have opposite requirements. They need temperate conditions with mild winters. If you grow an apple tree in Florida or oranges in New York, they don't stand a chance. The conditions needed to fulfill their potential just aren't quite right.

These fruits require the right conditions to grow and mature and ideal conditions to deliver perfect fruit. Suppose you commit to bringing your orange tree indoors for several months, with suitable soil and the right amount of sun and water. In that case, you can grow oranges in New York, but the tree will never grow to its potential with the limitations you have put on it. Your purpose is no different.

YOU WON'T BE LIVING IN YOUR PURPOSE AND SEEING IT COME TO LIFE IF YOU ARE DOING IT YOUR WAY, WITH YOUR RULES AND YOUR OWN PLANS OR AGENDA.

The walls and barriers we make create an atmosphere that we are comfortable within, that we control; we can really mess up how our purpose should be played out if we allow ourselves to get in the way.

REFLECTION SECTION

NOTES:

_____

_____

_____

_____

_____

_____

_____

_____

_____

_____

_____

_____

_____

_____

_____

_____

_____

2

INSECURITIES

First, we are created in God's image, as written in Genesis 1:26-27. "Then God said, 'Let Us make man in Our image, according to Our likeness; and let them rule over the fish of the sea and over the birds of the sky and over the cattle and over all the earth, and over every creeping thing that creeps on the earth.'"

God has given us a lot of power, authority, and responsibility to fulfill the mission given to us only. This means by living a life with God leading us; anything is possible.

Everything in the Bible has been written with a purpose: to show us life lessons, the ways we should live, God's great love for us, and also to show us what happens when we don't have faith enough to believe or obey Him.

Today, we have social media (pick your platform); so many of them show us what everyone looks like according to their best pictures, videos, etc. This may give you a false impression of them being all together. At their best they reinforce how inadequate you think you are in regards to what you're watching, what you don't have, how much money you are lacking, etc. A lot of users on these platforms end up using them as highlight reels and others use it to brag, but we end up interpreting them as what we are not, fueling our insecurities. We don't often see the struggles from the shadows of these highlight reels that reveal their battles in the background to release a perfect post. The struggle is more common than shown. Some people are just more talented at hiding their insecurities than facing them. These platforms are all right when enjoyed for what they are, to celebrate the great trick, new song, their talents displayed at their best. Fight the urge to be insecure in the moment, remind yourself that this is just a celebration of what they have accomplished through their hard work, not what you are not. You may be able to do some of these things, perhaps even better, or you might be just as talented at whatever they are showcasing for view. Remember, you cannot compare your beginnings to someone else's final product, their final delivery of what they are proud of doing. They could be viewing your life with the same insecurity that you are displaying or feeling. People tend to compare themselves to what everyone else is doing and that is damaging to your purpose. Comparing yourselves to others is often one of the biggest distractions you will face in your life.

Insecurity is a byproduct, an afterthought, or a symptom that is often caused by what we are faced with, challenged by, and even haunted by daily.

You may know the story of David and Goliath and when David received the anointing to lead Israel as king. His father thought David was insignificant because he was the youngest son, a farmhand, just out taking care of the sheep, etc.

Let's go back to the beginning of the story. David was just a kid chosen to tend the sheep and hold the lowly job of being a shepherd. Later on in the book we are going to talk about how important the role of being a shepherd is really is.

As a group of people, the Israelites turned their backs on God and more people wanted a king to protect them from attacks by the Philistines. Also, everyone else had a king and they wanted one as well. So, God gave His people the Israelites what they wanted, a king. Sometimes God will give us what we want even though it might not be what we need. We convince ourselves that it is the only way and refuse to wait on what God has for us; we can only see it this way. Walking in and owning your purpose allows you to follow God's heart, not yours. Our hearts will deceive us and steer us wrong every time. God can give us the desires of our hearts when we seek wisdom and guidance from Him. When you seek God, sometimes your personal desires will change and develop to work within God's purpose for you. Having God lead us is so much better than having God co-sign on our desires. After all the noise that the Israelites were sending about needing to be like all the other groups of people, God then gave Samuel specific directions on where and when he would find the anointed one, the one that would fulfill what they wanted as a king.

When Samuel found Saul, he looked the part but was anything but a leader. Saul found out the purpose of his life but never claimed it, didn't own it, and often ran from it. Saul was tall, strong, and handsome; he easily filled the ideal look of a leader.

In 1 Samuel 9:21 NLT, Saul replied, "But I'm only from the tribe of Benjamin, the smallest tribe in Israel, and my family is the least important of all the families of that tribe! Why are you talking like this to me?" Saul was full of reasons why he couldn't fulfill his purpose. Self-doubt, upbringing, everything he wasn't. This position is so easy to take when you don't trust in the One who designed you and created you to be who you are. Saul was comfortable complaining he wasn't from the right family, that he came from the smallest tribe in Israel; he just couldn't believe the prophet. He was convinced that nothing big or important could come from what he assigned insignificance to. God will often call people to do things that don't make sense with our limitations on thinking.

Saul stood out among his tribe and amongst the Israelites. The Bible says he was the most handsome and tallest in the land. Saul definitely looked the part. When I was a child, I was often the tallest in whatever circle I was in, and with that, people would treat me differently. I appeared older, so my parents would usually hold me to an older child's standards and behaviors, which was difficult for a very hyper, busy kid who needed to know how everything worked and what every light switch did. I was not able to always fulfill the expectations placed on me because I wasn't ready for what they thought I could handle. When Saul heard this information from Samuel, he was doubtful, unsure, and could only focus on what he wasn't. Sometimes, we let our "I can't" get way more significant than our "I can." We get insecure and tell ourselves that we will never fulfill what it is we're being told we will do. Insecurity is such a massive factor in fulfilling your purpose and the belief that you have what you need to carry out what it is that God has called you to do.

INSECURITY IS SIMPLY THE BIGGEST LIE THAT YOU CAN CONVINCE YOURSELF OF.

The devil, the enemy, whatever you choose to call him, loves that you choose to be in doubt and waver from your calling. Nothing is more detrimental to the devil and his agenda than someone who is secure in who God called them to be and is acting in faith, living out their purpose, owning it and living out a life that God has called them to.

I can relate to Saul's insecurities. When I was growing up and even until very recently, I was constantly searching for approval and recognizing self-importance. I was insecure in my abilities and struggling with the idea that I was called and capable of doing something, anything more prominent than I could see the beginning, middle and end of. Don't get me wrong, I could and still can dream really big, but that is where I unfortunately would let it die out. My imagination was on fire. I was always envisioning big things, big impossible things that I just dreamed about doing, and then I would let them go, because I couldn't get my courage and momentum to carry me forward. Thinking of the things that I let die in me that might have been needed to be fulfilled or released is sad to me, but I know that God is not done with me. I know that we serve a God that can fulfill all of those impossible things that we dream and help us with the ability to accomplish what He has called us for. The need to be told someone was proud of me, or "Wow, good job" was validation of my efforts, but then I would convince myself that they were only saying that to appease me. Even if I outperformed the majority, I was confident that I wasn't enough and that it was only a matter of time until someone would tell me so. I got praise, but all I heard was that I could have done better. I should've gotten a higher score. I would be the highest score, and yet all I heard was, "Are you okay with that? Are you all right missing the mark?" I wore these scores and phrases like clothing. I felt like it became my identity, which couldn't be further from the truth. Your identity should not be in a number, or what you wear, or what you drive, or the school you go to.

The Bible says in Romans 12:4-5, "For just as we have many members in one body and all the members do not have the same purpose, so we, who are many, are one body in Christ, and individually members one of another."

Your identity is in Christ, not what we assign or let someone else assign to us. Our insecurity tells us that we are not enough, unqualified, too simple, too ugly, too old, too used, too addicted. The list goes on and on. We need to silence the voice of insecurity we are listening to and speak over what we are hearing. For example, "I am enough, I am a child of God, I was created and called for a purpose, I am willing to do whatever God asks me to do. I can write a book even though English was not a class I enjoyed." (Too personal, I guess) We can choose to listen to the negative, or we can fight the noise and speak these positives loudly and purposefully till they take root. You will still feel the urge to listen to "what you are not," but you have to respond and change the narrative immediately. You may find it beneficial to write down a list of what you are or what positive claims you can recite that will encourage you. Now get writing. It can start out as a vision, something that God showed you yet to be confirmed, but these are faith statements, things you are believing for.

Habakkuk 2:2 says, "Then the Lord answered me and said, 'Record the vision and inscribe it on tablets, That the one who reads it may run.'" To simplify, write down what you believe, whether it's a dream or a vision, who God is calling you to be, and watch it happen.

WRITE SOME OF YOUR DECLARATIONS/VISIONS HERE:

_____

_____

_____

_____

_____

_____

_____

_____

_____

_____

_____

_____

_____

_____

_____

I always felt that I was so different because I was taller, went to church, didn't have the most incredible brands of clothes to wear, and looked at things so differently than most. My value was assigned to the things I had and what I wore, not to the value of what I had to offer. For me, being a very random thinker was scary and stressful because I knew it was so different from how other people saw life. I always approached life as half full instead of half empty, always trying to see what things were and not what they weren't. Maybe you have the opposite view as me.

My fear of disappointing anyone close to me was terrifying and controlling, and only fueled the insecurities more. It didn't matter if it was a teacher, parent, any adult, my boss, my team, my employees, the waitress that asked me to repeat myself because I talked too quietly. It may not have been all true, but when you are focused on what you interpret and not on what God tells you, crazy stuff happens. I missed out on friend opportunities, positions, jobs, etc., because my insecurities held me back. Imagine the impact I could have made if I didn't let those thoughts win. I remember when I was in second grade, and we got a new student in the class who was deaf. No one else in the class knew sign language, and they asked if anyone would like to learn. This young lady's family moved in next door to us, and I thought it would be great to take the lessons to learn sign language and make a new friend. The day the classes started, I was the only boy who went to the classes to better myself and learn to talk to my new friend. Talk

32

about an insecurity-building setup. The whole class picked on me because it was such a different thing to do. A boy taking a class with all girls was just weird. This event in my life definitely impacted what I chose to do throughout school and whatever I decided to do next. It formed a path that I stayed on whether it came to church, school plays, school TV, even doing a presentation in class, I would do just enough to get by. I let insecurity keep me in the crowd and not to step out into current and against the grain.

There were many things in life I didn't go do because I thought someone would be disappointed, or left out, or judging me. Even though I felt left out constantly, not being invited to do anything, not included in the current conversations, being too insecure to join hurt only me. It broke my confidence and the value I assigned myself, knowing now that I might have had what they needed to hear. Just maybe I could have added value. Perhaps they would have helped me to realize what I needed or what I was missing out on.

Like Saul, I had insecurities that controlled me, shaped me, and led me to believe a lot of things, to disqualify myself into thinking that I would never be good enough, or what people wanted me to be, let alone what God wanted me to be. I believed God could not want me to do something like this or that. God had to be wrong. I know now that God can't be false or make the wrong choices as to who He calls to do what. Your purpose lies in what God has created you to fulfill. It will blow your mind, it might even make you go, "God, really? Me, God? I'm the only one that can fill this purpose?" God gave you this ability to execute the way He intended you to do it.

To make this easier to understand; this is how I break it down.

DON'T LET WHERE YOU CAME FROM OR WHO YOU ARE OR USED TO BE DISCREDIT YOU FROM WHAT GOD HAS FOR YOU.

We are created in His image; we are given what we need to make it through each day and to fulfill and own the purpose He gave us. In a way, having insecurities in who God made you is basically telling God He got it wrong, or you're having trouble believing what God said. Not knowing how to fulfill our God-given purpose is part of the journey. If we knew how to do it or it comes super easy, then it doesn't take faith in God to get it done. It could not be God's plan, just something we thought of, if we could make it happen by our own will and abilities. We need to be ready to be tested and challenged and stretched to be able to focus and succeed in God's purpose for our lives.

God wants to be our enough, to be the strength we need, but this passage shows us that God listens to the hearts and cries of his people. 1 Samuel 10: 20-23.

Samuel gathered all the tribes of Israel together to choose a leader using a method called drawing a lot. Lots are just a set number of rocks or small objects put into a bag and only one is marked differently and the person that chooses the different one becomes the winner or the chosen one. Ever watched that show where they are all stranded on the island and have to eat barely anything and do strenuous games and challenges? They have to do this at different times on different seasons of the show. The tribe of Benjamin was chosen and then Saul was selected from among his people. Saul then went into hiding because he could not believe that he was the chosen one. His insecurities led him into the shadows, from his purpose assigned from God.

Saul could not be found anywhere. God then told Samuel that he was hiding among the baggage of all the travelers, so when Samuel brought Saul out, he said, "This is the man that is chosen by God as your ing because he is like no one else." They began to cheer for Saul, "Long live the king!" I can imagine at this point Saul looked the part, appearing to be the one, but he was terrified because he felt so unqualified.

God will sometimes give you what your heart cries out

for, not always what you need. The Israelites were really focused on image and any person other than Saul would most likely not have met the image they thought they needed to be a king. You will not always be everyone's ideal image of what God has asked you to do. Be careful of who you share your purpose with when it might not be the right time, because not everyone will see it, understand it, or support it. This will only fuel insecurity and cause it to take hold in your life. You have to surround yourself with people who will support you even if your purpose doesn't make much sense. If you know it's God given, you will need encouragement to move forward.

I am a retail manager for a living. Having done retail for a long time, I've held many titles and positions over my career, but throughout a lot of it I needed to show that I was capable of being the best. I pushed through challenges and obstacles to stand out for all the good reasons. Many times, all it took was my insecurity of failing or being thought less of to drive my success.

I have accomplished a lot throughout my career, building good teams, routines, and producing solid results in all the roles I have held. I have faced a couple of rough times through this journey and can remember distinctly hearing the simple, loud word "Disappointed" coming from my leader's voice, and that's all it took. "Disappointed" was a trigger word for me that would fuel my insecurities and push me in the direction I needed to go because I was not too fond of the thought of letting someone down. I wore that word as if I wore a t-shirt that said "Disappointment." It was my label that I assigned myself. I was going to give the best I had in me somehow. My insecure self took me to the top of the ranks in performance and helped me receive many offers for jobs and roles that scared me, but I took them and did well because of my fear of not being the best. Living this lie is tough. See, I had the ability within me to do the job, but I let fear take the lead instead of having faith that "I got this." The times I struggled hard were when fear took me out of my routines and refocused me on doing it all myself. You will struggle to be a successful leader when you choose to take on all the tasks and responsibilities yourself. You are only as good as the people you lead. Insecure people tend to lead by themselves rather than with others or a team. I have seen it over and over again, leaders that are really good people but are the only ones working really hard and they just never get where they are trying to go. They get so frustrated because no one can do it like them, or as quickly as them. If you want to be free from insecurity, it is truly about letting go, letting your team grow by doing it and in turn learning how to lead others to get things done. Insecure people also tend to need to be the smartest person in the room. This is exactly the wrong approach. I have found that my insecurities are less in control when I constantly challenge myself to find circles of people where I am always learning. When you let go and always strive to make your team smarter than you, you are still growing. I want nothing more than for my children to take off from my ceiling as their floor. I love all the new stuff they tell me and how excited they get to know something dad doesn't.

Sometimes I pushed my insecurities out of my focus, then other times I gave in to them, and they pushed me over. It's really hard to process the moments I gave into those insecurities and other times I did not, but it comes down to whether or not I could see the path or if I had to go into it blindly. In some cases, my insecurities led me to success down a path I could see and trust, not the way I was intended to go, but there was a significant problem with doing it my way. I was so depressed and frustrated and lacked joy during much of this time because insecurity will rob you of your joy if you let it. There is an emptiness when you do things your way, not the intended way. It's that feeling that you have so much of what you pursued, and yet you feel so empty.

When I was sixteen, I went bungee jumping with a bunch of friends. Not all of us did it, and honestly, I wasn't sure what I was going to do. So, I signed the waivers, gave payment to the cashier, and looked up at this colossal structure that I had to climb. Yes, there was no elevator or lift; it was a 165' ladder that had breaks so you would switch sides so just in case you were to fall, you wouldn't fall that far. I got to the top of the climb with knees wobbling and walked across the platform that was swaying back and forth in the light wind. I sat down, and the guy proceeded to take this bungee cord and attach it to my feet. This process blew my mind. They take a white towel, wrap it around your ankles, take this giant rubber band (bungee cord) that has a loop at the end, and with the loop over your ankles they twist it a couple of times and you are hooked up, ready to go. The attendant helped me up and I was standing at the edge looking down over this shallow hole filled with water that looked like a soup bowl from this height. He said to me, "You can jump whenever you are ready." So I jumped. It was one of the greatest moments I had encountered up to this point of my life. I think only one of my other friends did it that day with me. When I got down to the ground, the adrenaline was still pumping through my body; I felt like I ignored my fear, challenged my insecurity, and pushed through with success. Everyone including the attendant came to me and was like "You just jumped! You didn't even hesitate." Looking back, was this a shocking behavior for people to observe from me? In a moment, my victory over insecurity was gone. My insecurity now was, "Wow, Jeremy was not calculated, not planned out, didn't know the outcome but just went for it."

DON'T LET VICTORIES IN YOUR LIFE CREATE NEW INSECURITIES.

They will creep in if you let them, any chance they can. My friends probably had no idea that was the processing I was going through. I didn't talk to many people about the insecurities that I was dealing with. I thought I was concealing my struggles from them, yet their reactions showed me that my responses are telling a story that everyone can see.

Sometimes, my insecurities have led me to over-learn, over-analyze, over-study, and over-prepare so there was no chance for me to fail, not realizing that there is purpose in pain and failing. We are imperfect, and we are need someone to fill in the gaps. Someone that can go before us to make the fall hurt less. Jesus is the someone who is there to catch us. We tend to often fall on our own, because when things are working, we tend not to lean in to Jesus first. Insecurity can make you want something or to be offered something that you were not ready for and you're often not willing to blame yourself. It's really the opposite of purpose. When your purpose is revealed, you have to be willing to take the chance and say, "God, I don't know why, but I get it. I will head in the direction I think You are telling me to go and I will let You course correct me as you see fit."

BACK TO SAUL:

Saul was told to kill the all the Amalekites and all their livestock. He felt that God was wrong, and he had a different idea of what should be done. He straight up disobeyed God's direction and kept the king and all the best livestock alive. Saul wasn't willing to follow the direction the Lord gave him because it couldn't possibly be correct. He might have thought, "Why would I waste all this great livestock and kill the king? I can find favor with others when they see I spared him." Saul failed to follow his purpose and direction and it led to many unnecessary events in the future. He made excuses that he didn't kill the livestock because it would make great sacrifices, but in reality, his obedience was the sacrifice required of him. Sometimes we make decisions because we can't see the point or the reason why God is asking us to do such a thing. Just because your purpose or calling doesn't make sense now, you still need to make the choice to be obedient.

Saul's lack of understanding his purpose and God-given instruction grew to his lack of trust from God. Your God given purpose is key to getting it done through Christ and being trusted with what you need to own your purpose. If you are trusted to execute a plan then it's key to complete your assignment with the means that God has assigned you. Saul's attempt to accomplish this task ended in a resounding and catastrophic flop.

This led to the following conversation between the Lord and Samuel in 1 Samuel 15:11-12:

> *" 'I regret that I have made Saul king, for he has turned back from following Me and has not carried out My commands.' And Samuel was distressed and cried out to the Lord all night. Samuel rose early in the morning to meet Saul; and it was told to Samuel, saying, 'Saul came to Carmel, and behold, he set*

up a monument for himself, then turned and proceeded on down to Gilgal.'"

Often insecurity can lead a man to take credit for everything he does that he thinks is right and he blames others for his own failures along the way. It can cause him to think that building a monument would address his shortcomings and fulfill the emptiness he felt because he knew he was disobedient and didn't follow what God had laid out for him to complete. Saul was an ideal candidate for the look and stature of a king, according to what the Israelites thought they needed and wanted. The key word being what the people "wanted," not what they really "needed." See, God wanted to be their King, to be enough for them. Yet the people where envious of the other nations because they all had something that they wanted: a king, a leader that they could see in person, right in front of them.

It's like when a dog has a toy they appear to not be able to live without, until you pull a different toy out from somewhere and then they need that one immediately. Jealousy and envy will quickly rob you of the joy you currently have in life. You can be really good at something until you watch someone else do it a little better, and then if you let your insecurity take control you immediately devalue what you have or are able to do. I have done this my whole life. With cars, bikes, motorcycles, boats, fishing equipment, whatever it was. Insecurities can cost you a lot of money and they have for me several times. In 2006, I went to look at new vehicles, and as usual I wore a black t-shirt with paint on it, ripped up jeans, and a hat. I did not look like I had it together but approached a salesman and asked for assistance. He looked me up and down and said, "I'm busy, I'll see if I can find someone to help you." Then he proceeded to grab a lady who had just started that day and sent her over to me. My insecurities definitely got the best of me, because I was thinking, "How dare you judge me, assuming I don't have what I need to buy a new truck?" Meanwhile, the truck I was driving was only 10 months old. So, I told her loud enough for everyone to hear, including the salesman who was not doing anything and said he was too busy to help me, to please show me the most expensive truck on the lot and I would buy it today. I really showed him, didn't I? I left with a gigantic payment, a really nice truck, and yet my insecurities won. So did the car dealership. The original salesman was so mad for missing out on the sale. The new saleswomen, however, could not have been more excited. My insecurities and stupidity landed her a large commission check. Insecurity will make you regret the decisions you make because you are being robbed from what could have been, if you had not let your insecurities lead the way.

At this point, Saul doesn't know that his anointing is being passed on and becomes faced with a new challenge. Goliath.

SEE, AN INSECURE PERSON WILL MANAGE HIS PEOPLE FROM BEHIND INSTEAD OF LEADING THE WAY FROM THE FRONT.

He will stay behind the trouble and the dangers and the obstacles, shying away from his purpose and responsibilities that he is faced with. If Saul had only allowed God to lead him, so in turn he could lead the armies of the living God, Saul would have been on the right track, living out his calling. Saul already had all he needed to defeat Goliath, yet he let his insecurities lead.

I used to be just like this. It always had to be my way; I was the reason things went well, me and me alone. God eventually allowed me to see it was Him that led me to those successes, that He was the reason for my success, all these things had been accomplished by His aid. It is not possible that I could do all this on my own. It's like this: If you believe that you are living in your purpose but it only takes your own strength and it's easy street, then you're not living your purpose. It is way bigger than you can handle without God. Your purpose will be what God can trust you with, with guidance from Him and trusting in God daily that your steps are ordered by Him.

Insecurities, although common amongst us all, are different for different people. What makes me insecure might not make you insecure; what makes you insecure today might not make you insecure tomorrow. Insecurities will affect you differently in different seasons of your life. Many times throughout my life, I was insecure about how well I did in school, how successful I was at work, whether it was a very unsuccessful paper route, cooking burgers on the grill at the restaurant, or leading the way as a manager in a few different companies. Insecurity doesn't often make sense, because it is usually fueled by thoughts and concerns that you make up. There is nothing like living in a lie daily to make you doubt your value and your successes.

EXAMPLES:

Getting top grades consistently but always feeling that you are just not enough; you are thinking that everyone around you is disappointed because you're not enough.

Ranking top scores in your company but thinking that every day you are going to be let go because of who knows what.

Both of these examples used to fuel my success. I always worried about the impressions I left, so I was super focused on excelling at what I did. Insecurities are just a form of self-manipulation, convincing yourself of a false identity that is created by your assumptions or always driving yourself from false information that you have convinced yourself to be true.

You can stop fighting and hating yourself in the shadows, trying to figure it all out yourself, and start leaning on Jesus to lead you out of the shadows of insecurities and into the light. When we trust in our Lord and the power He has for us, all our insecurities can be erased. This doesn't mean that they won't show up from time to time, but we do have better processes to deal with them. Jesus can take away those insecurities and turn them into truths. I'm good at that. I can do this, I will get where I am going. I will accomplish all that God has called me to.

In Exodus 3: 11-12, "But Moses said to God, 'Who am I, that I should go to Pharaoh, and that I should bring the sons of Israel out of Egypt?' And He said, 'Certainly I will be with you, and this shall be the sign to you that it is I who have sent you: when you have brought the people out of Egypt, you shall worship God at this mountain.'"

Moses' insecurity leads him to tell God that he was not enough. Moses had a stutter and felt he was not equipped to be what he was being called to do, But God says simply, "I will be with you." If we can live in this space knowing that God is with us at all times, our insecurities are made small and become insignificant. They cannot rule our lives.

Final thought: insecurity can keep the real you buried

in the shadows to the point that God will use someone else to do what you were called for. Israel's insecurities about not having a king led to God giving them exactly what they thought and saw a king as, and what the people were calling for. Saul was not God's first choice to lead Israel as the first king, but God answered the people's wish to be led the same way as all the nations all around them. God wanted to be their King, and it was His desire to give them the king they needed with David when the timing was God's, not theirs.

GOD HAS BEEN SETTING YOUR PATH FOR YOU EVEN BEFORE YOU COULD RECOGNIZE YOUR PURPOSE.

David was anointed and then went back to work for his father. Being secure in what God made you makes it okay to go back to tend to the sheep or be an errand boy running food to your brothers on the battlefield. It's okay to keep cooking French fries till it's time to move into what's next. Living beyond your insecurities leads you to God's will for your life. God may reveal what's next or where you will end up, but most often the path is not clear.

In Philippians 4:6-9 NIV it says: "Do not be anxious about anything, but in every situation, by prayer and petition, with thanksgiving, present your requests to God. And the peace of God, which transcends all understanding, will guard your hearts and your minds in Christ Jesus. Finally, brothers and sisters, whatever is true, whatever is noble, whatever is right, whatever is pure, whatever is lovely, whatever is admirable—if anything is excellent or praiseworthy—think about such things. Whatever you have learned or received or heard from me, or seen in me—put it into practice. And the God of peace will be with you."

WHAT INSECURITIES DO YOU NEED TO FINALLY PUT IN GOD'S HANDS?

_____

_____

_____

_____

WHAT IS KEEPING YOU FROM TRUSTING WHAT GOD'S PLAN HAS FOR YOU?

_____

_____

_____

_____

My joy was missing for a long time, until God made it clear

to me that He has me, He has it, I just needed to accept that as my reality.

Committing to spending daily time with God will change everything. It has for me. What a difference when you are focused on consecrating your time with God, getting to know Him better. When you make time for what you want to make time for, that area of your life gets fed. It grows, gets stronger, smarter, and more focused than it was. There are some of us out there who show that we can quote every movie we ever watched or remember every character of a card game with all their stats and abilities, but can't name five books of the Bible. Most things you run into head on with five hours of whatever it is will just burn you out. Start out small at first and then you will realize that you cannot give God enough time. Five minutes a day with the Bible and prayer will quickly grow when you start to feel God using what you are reading and developing those areas of your life.

I have always been an insecure person because I have spent so much time being the person that I thought everyone needed, and hiding a lot of who I was. That is where this book is coming from. I hope to help readers grow and change and live in confidence to pursue their God-given purpose, to own what God is calling them to.

When you start to feel the triggers of insecurities come up—and oh, they will—grab the Bible, pray or call out to God. When you need God, you do not need to be formal; yelling HELP often works well. Call a friend; reach out to someone who will not condemn you. A good friend will be challenging you often, and that is a good thing. Seeking someone to help you see what is real and what is self-induced will often lead to clarity.

My fear of failing caused me to over think, over plan, and over process to the point that it stole the joy from some things I was once so excited about. Things like musical instruments, drawing, sports and schoolwork. I did well in school, but I didn't strive to take any extra or advanced classes because of the "what if." What if I tried something complicated and I didn't pull it off or succeed at it? How could I live with that? It's sad looking back at how much I would have benefited from having just one person push me further in all aspects of my life, but I really didn't have that. I had some friends, but I just didn't seek many friendships because the real me might be seen. People needed all the real me, but after hearing so many times that I was too much, too hyper, need to calm down etc., it starts to become your identity. I missed out on a lot of life for fear that I would fail. I was once told by my then girlfriend (now wife) that when we go for a ride with her parents that they don't have conversations and talk as much as I do in the car. I let it go, but it really did bother me. I was so used to hearing things like this my whole life that I let these insecurities shape what and who I was. Just to let you know, this is not the case anymore; they fully know what craziness I'm bringing to the party. I can't hold back; I have to be myself if I don't want stifle the gifts God gave me.

Stepping into God's will and purpose for you will take a leap of faith; it will challenge you to a point that you cannot plan for much at all. Planning and learning are really good things to do, when you know what you are doing and what direction you have to head. Sometimes your purpose will begin to reveal when you are equipped for what God is challenging you with and you start walking in a direction.

YOU MAY HEAD NORTH AND EVENTUALLY GOD WILL TAKE YOU SOUTH, BUT DON'T DOUBT IT'S PART OF THE PROCESS.

In Genesis 1: 26-28 it states: "Then God said, 'Let Us make man in Our image, according to Our likeness; let them have dominion over the fish of the sea, over the birds of the air, and over the cattle, over all the earth and over every creeping thing that creeps on the earth.' So, God created man in their own image; in the image of God, He created them; male and female He created them. Then God blessed them, and God said to them, 'Be fruitful and multiply; fill the earth and subdue it; have dominion over the fish of the sea, over the birds of the air, and over every living thing that moves on the land.'"

Have confidence that you are strictly who God has intended you to be and begin to let those insecurities leave you. Don't let them rob of you of what you are here on earth for this time to complete. Your purpose is waiting on you, to be fulfilled in God's intended way.

REFLECTION SECTION

WHAT IN YOUR LIFE HAS MADE YOU
INSECURE?

_____

_____

_____

_____

WHAT DO YOU NEED TO NOT LET
CONTROL YOUR DECISIONS AND
ACTIONS?

_____

_____

_____

_____

NOTES:

_____

_____

_____

_____

3

THE SHEPHERD IN ME

At some point in your life, you will be a leader of something, or maybe you have already stepped up to be a leader. You have to lead. Whether it's school, a job, in your family, or within a group of friends, eventually you will be called to lead in some capacity.

A shepherd is a unique leader not typically viewed as an essential part of society in the old days. Although a shepherd would care for one of the most valuable assets an owner could have had back in the day, the shepherd was often viewed as lowly and unimportant. The shepherd would be so in tune with his flock that they would know him by voice and be comforted by his presence. Shepherds rarely left the flock because of their connection with the sheep.

There arc so many exciting things about sheep. They

have discovered that when sheep are sheared, it is better to keep their faces unshorn so that when they go back into the pen with the rest of the flock they are recognized, and the other sheep are not scared by the different-looking animal that has rejoined them. It is so interesting to me to think that they are such simple animals. A sheep will often do whatever the one next to it does; it will mimic or copy its flockmate's behavior. This is why you often see sheep being moved to the left or the right by a dog or shepherd who gets one or two moving and the others simply follow. If a sheep gets scared it can infect the whole flock with fear and they can do crazy things. If one is spooked and jumps off a cliff, not really thinking about what it just did, the rest of the flock will follow suit and jump as well. A shepherd could lose the entire flock if one gets out of line. It is crazy to think this can happen with sheep, but as a society, we do things like this every day. We are just sheep that tend to go along with whatever is popular, whatever is the current trend. Think fashion, music, trends (social media), etc. That is why marketing is so important. If they can get your attention in about 11 seconds or less, they have probably got you. I heard once that the most time people spend watching the same online video is a maximum of 11 seconds. Those who make it past that point are hooked and most likely will finish whatever they are watching. It's so important that we are mindful of what captures us or our attention.

The shepherd would carry a staff with a hook at one end of it while keeping watch over the sheep. This staff had many purposes. He could use it to hook the sheep to pull it or lead it to him at a safe distance without spooking the sheep, in turn startling the whole flock. Even though the shepherd was there to watch the sheep, he would have to live with them, so they were confident about who their shepherd was and who would protect them. Shepherds would spend their whole day and night amongst the sheep, whether it was rain or shine, winter or summer. His focus was protecting the sheep for the owner. The landowners would often build a pen of stone, basically a fenced-in area, and the shepherd would sleep in front of the entrance to protect the sheep from leaving or anything coming in to attack them. Sheep had to learn the hard way at times, also. If a sheep wandered away from the flock and got lost the shepherd would use the staff and sometimes hit the back leg of a sheep, often breaking its leg so it couldn't run away again. The sheep would become very dependent on the shepherd. The sheep would associate the pain with being away from its shepherd, so it would choose to stay close. Ever see that picture of Jesus portrayed carrying a sheep on His shoulders? I think you get what the picture is probably trying to tell us now. This pain the sheep experienced would cause the sheep to have to rely on the shepherd to survive.

The shepherd would ensure that the sheep would be able to eat and be protected. It sounds a lot like the relationship that you get to have with Jesus. We were all broken to the extent of being lost, and yet when we accept Jesus in our hearts as our Savior it is like a sheep returning unto a shepherd, healing through our brokenness, knowing that the true Shepherd is protecting us. It says that the shepherd will leave the flock of 99 to retrieve the one. We are the ones that Jesus came and died for. He picked us up to protect and care for us when we chose to have Him as our Shepherd.

In 1 Samuel, we learn about David, the youngest son of Jesse. David was out in the fields being a shepherd when Samuel was led by God to the house of Jesse to anoint the king of Israel. When Jesse presented his sons to Samuel, he didn't even bother calling on David, who was out in the fields. David was small and insignificant compared to his brothers. Back in these times, the largest share of the inheritance and property was reserved for the oldest son. David was assigned the task of taking care of the sheep, a job that would be given to a servant or enslaved person. David, being the youngest, was dismissed as being not important enough to join the meeting with Samuel.

When Samuel met with Jesse, he asked Jesse to bring his sons to him, and the Lord said to Samuel, "Don't look upon the appearance or height of their stature, because I have rejected them. I look at the heart." One after another Jesse called his sons, only for them to all be turned down. As the seventh son passed Samuel and was rejected, Samuel asked, "Do you have more than seven sons?" Samuel knew and trusted what God told him and was confused. So reluctantly sending for David as Samuel requested nothing occurred or would be continued till David was brought in from the fields. I'm sure David was suntanned, dirty, and smelled horrible because he lived among the animals. David walked into the room and as Samuel approached David, lifting the vessel of oil over David's head, it began pouring oil over his head and Samuel knew that he found who God sent him to see. I would be willing to bet the room went dead quiet in shock at this moment. How could someone so young, as David, and opposes what the opposite of what the idea of a leader should be, be the chosen one?

WHAT YOU ARE AND WHERE YOU COME FROM DOES NOT DICTATE WHAT GOD HAS FOR YOU. YOU ARE SET APART FOR A SPECIFIC PURPOSE THAT ONLY YOU CAN FULFULL AS INTENDED.

You are set apart for a specific purpose that only you can fulfill as intended.

David was anointed by Samuel to become the king of Israel, but as a boy he went back to his current purpose, shepherding the sheep in the fields. David didn't demand that things change immediately, that he move into royal status. He knew that his purpose at that time was taking care of his father's sheep and went back out to living out his current purpose. His obedience to his father led to the interaction with Samuel. You may know your purpose, but God will show you the time and place when the following steps are coming. I took photography in high school, and I learned that the timing of exposing a film strip to develop a picture was super important. The teacher went through several strips of film teaching the process, taking the proper steps to make the film come out correctly. With the wrong timing, it will not be as intended, either overexposed or not enough. If the negatives are not correct, the picture will not turn out the way the photographer envisioned it.

In Jeremiah 1:5, God says, "Before I formed you in your mother's womb, I knew you; before you were born, I sanctified you; and I ordained you a prophet to the nations." God has a plan and purpose for our lives. When we become in tune with the plan of God and spend time with Him, we learn the purpose and plan God has for us.

As David's story continues, he comes face to face with Goliath, because David's father Jesse asked him one day to take lunch out to the battlefield. David's obedience to his father put David in the right place to take the following steps of his anointing, leading him towards becoming the king. David's time as a shepherd prepared him for his impending battle with Goliath. David fought against lions and bears; the text says that he went after them to protect the sheep, tearing their jaws open and killing them.

David heard the Philistine giant Goliath taunting and ridiculing the Israeli army. Immediately, something rose up in him and he insisted on going out to challenge the giant. David's oldest brother Eliab verbally attacked David by saying his role of shepherd was insignificant. "Who is watching our few sheep? You came here with your insolence and wickedness in your heart." It makes you wonder if this shows the true heart of Eliab the brother. Maybe this is why he wasn't the chosen one of God, as David was. David was obedient and brought the cheese and crackers (basically) and his brothers treated him like this. Living your life as a shepherd isn't glamourous and not everyone will appreciate all you do. Often the favor you have been shown will cause people to lash out and direct frustration your way! David was God's plan all along to be the first king of Israel, but instead of letting God be their Shepherd, they took off complaining and demanding a different direction than what was intended.

Saul, the king of Israel, insisted that David wear his personal armor, but David (I'm assuming as nicely as possible) shook off the armor and said it just wouldn't work. It was probably like my four-year-old putting my clothes on and expecting to do all the crazy stuff he does and he can't function. He cannot move, jump, or run the way he usually does, so he steps out of what isn't currently intended for him. David went out to face the giant like he was going to the fields to meet any other day with his father's sheep, slingshot and a few smooth stones from the brook in his possession. David called out as written in 1 Samuel 17:26, "After all, who is this heathen uncircumcised Philistine to defy the armies of the one Living God?" I can hear the armies on both sides gasping at the sound of this young man calling out a giant in front of his army and their enemies. I imagine his voice was cracking, and only the soldiers in the first couple of rows could hear him shout. People in the back were yelling, "What did he say? What is he thinking?" What an insult that David went at this giant with. This powerful statement that David proclaimed in front of everyone led to the moment he prepared for. He sent the stone flying into the air and sinking into Goliath's head. Not only did he take out the giant, but he stood over him, picked up Goliath's sword, and cut off his head with his own sword. Sounds like a major statement to me. I'm sure David had the confidence that God was with him, shepherding him into the situation that was in front of him.

With the path that you are on, searching for and living out life to own your purpose will require you to live in a shepherd relationship with Jesus. In turn, it will prepare you to shepherd those around you. It allows you to keep your children safe, your friends to have someone to lean on, a group of people to know that they can go to you when they are in trouble or need guidance.

UNDERSTANDING YOUR RELATIONSHIP WITH JESUS WILL ALLOW YOU TO LIVE OUT BEING A SHEPHERD FOR OTHERS.

A pastor is a shepherd to the congregation, a teacher is a shepherd to their students, a parent to their children... it can go on forever. God has put them in a position of responsibility to lead their group of people, to learn the way Jesus intends us to live and to teach us the proper way to do math, or life lessons that we need to be successful in life.

Responsible parents shepherd their children because a child without guidance and course correction will be led astray from the focus a child needs. For example, if you don't teach your child to do dishes correctly (not missing spaghetti sauce stuck in the rivets of the saucepan or food between the tines of the forks) the dishes will be put away dirty. If you fix the situation yourself without teaching them, they may never learn how to do it right.

Throughout my life, I have been a leader in some capacity in almost everything I have done. I had a hard time not taking the lead when it came to projects, play time, what games we played as children, or who got to go first. You will find true leaders don't need to claim it or self-title themselves; it just organically happens. Many times leaders rise up and people just follow. If you exchange leader for shepherd, it makes more sense that people are in this role. A shepherd isn't afraid and is often the best servant in the room. They are willing to put their lives in the path of danger or go first to ensure that it is okay and safe for others. We would adventure through the woods as kids, always expecting to find something special or hidden, but I also had to lead the way. I can remember playing church and turning a large cardboard box upside down to make a preacher pedestal, opening up my Bible, and reciting the only verse I knew by heart as loud and commanding as I could, John 3:16 , "For God so loved the world, that he gave his only begotten Son…" When God gave us a shepherd in Jesus, He set up a way for us to have a relationship with the Father through His one and only SON. When Jesus was here in person on earth, people just flocked to Him. They moved and followed Him as a shepherd with his sheep. There are so many examples in the Bible where Jesus had crowds of people around Him.

In Matthew 14:13-21, Jesus has a shepherding moment with the 12 disciples and 5000 men with their wives and children. The people all followed Jesus to a place where He was going to try and seek solitude on hearing the news that John the Baptist had been beheaded. Jesus had gotten on a boat to travel away from the crowds, and when the people heard where He was going, they all traveled from the villages and cities to meet Him there. When Jesus saw all the people that had met Him, He felt compassion for them. He called for them to sit down around Him. Some of the disciples came to Jesus and said that the people were hungry and that they should be sent away so they could go and get themselves something to eat. Jesus spoke to the disciples and told them the people didn't need to go away; the disciples should feed them! A shepherd would never send his sheep off to eat without him. He provides what his flock needs. A disciple said to Jesus that they only had five loaves of bread and two fish, Jesus then asked for the food to be brought to Him. Now this isn't an endless supply of food; this is enough food to feed a couple of people a decent meal. But this Shepherd is not like any other. Jesus took the food, blessed it, and gave the food to the disciples so they could start handing it out. The disciples began to distribute the food and didn't hold back with any portion control. The Bible says that the people ate until they were filled. Immediately, this became a buffet unlike anyone had seen before. To think that people could eat as much as they wanted and not worry about the food running out! Experts say that there must have been over fifteen thousand people this day. The Bible only recorded the men in attendance but it states also there were women and children in the crowd. Now I don't know where the 12 baskets came from, but the disciples went around and picked up 12 full baskets of leftover bread and fish. Each of the disciples had a basket full of what originally was only five loaves of bread and two fish. I'm a fisherman, and in my hands two fish and five loaves of bread will not go far. This story shows the compassion of the Shepherd. Jesus as the Shepherd here reached His flock in their need. He gathered them together, had them sit around Him, and fed them spiritually and with food. He saw their desire to be in His presence. A shepherd needs to take care of himself as well. After the people were fed and the disciples collected all the food, Jesus sent the people away and then dismissed the disciples with orders to get in the boat and go to the other side of the lake.

As a leader, Jesus shows us accountability to His disciples and the people who came to see Him and heard what He had to say, and that He did nothing without reaching out to His Father. Did Jesus really have to pray over the bread before He broke it? I mean, He is God, but He still reached out to the Father in the moment of need. In a position of leadership, you will always be accountable to someone. In retail, an associate has a supervisor, supervisors have managers, managers have field leaders, there are corporate leaders and a board of directors. There are many branches on this leadership tree, but this demonstrates the levels of accountability. A shepherd has his sheep that he is accountable to be there for, to protect, lead, teach, and develop desired behaviors. Yet, he is accountable to the owner, or in David's situation his father.

Are there areas in your life where you have the role of shepherd? As a parent, you have the responsibility to keep your household safe. You have to train your children to do the right thing, act a certain way, and respect each other. You need to teach them how to handle difficult decisions, how to make the right choices, how to clean up after themselves, and the list goes on and on. If you are a student, you may be in the role of shepherd for your friends or other classmates. Think of it as a role model, demonstrating the behaviors that are desirable for a school setting. A teacher or counselor may assign you this role, or your personality may lead you into this position. Not all leaders are appointed; many of them rise to the occasion when something calls them into action. Maybe you never looked at yourself as a leader, but believe me, there is a shepherd in all of us.

Who is shepherding you? Do you have someone that you look up to or look to for guidance? Shepherding can look like a mentor relationship as well. We all have mentors that we look up to. Some of us have mentor relationships with people we may never meet. For example, you may have someone you watch weekly online, or listen to podcasts or different content. These are people that you trust and look up to and you emulate some of their behaviors that you observe and learn from. There are two sides to this, though. The construct of shepherding I've been talking about here is a positive one. However, you can consume content and examples from your mentors and adapt what you see and learn from them only to be led in the wrong direction, down a path you are not intended for. It is said that what you get around can get on you, and what you get on you gets in you, and eventually it will come out of you. So, if you are constantly around and taking in unhealthy content, it will ultimately come out. I always used to listen to music full of explicit content and eventually I talked just like it. I mean, the language that I used was just not appropriate for almost every setting I was in. However, I would clean it up around particular family members because I didn't want them to see the wreck I had become. One of the most significant changes I made in my life was the content that I was consuming. Now I read the Bible almost every day and consume God-centric content through preaching, podcasts, or worship music that drives me in the direction I want to go. It has become the loudest influence in my daily life, which allows God to open doors where walls were before. We are not bulletproof, and whether we are old or young we are constantly being influenced by what is going on around us. Make wise choices about the music you listen to, the podcasts you watch, and just the general content that you take in so you can make smart decisions about what you do, say, and how you live your life. Being accountable to yourself and close friends, family members, teachers, pastors, etc. will help shape who you become. You have to make the choices that will take you down the right path.

Do you reach out to someone when you need guidance, when you need help deciding what path to take? We are not designed to do life alone. We need to have a network of people in our lives who coach us and others we coach in return. We need people that will support the path we are taking and call us back when we take a wrong turn. Those special people in our lives that won't lead us off the cliff because we may not be able to see the implications of jumping currently. These people keep us going in the direction we feel called to go and don't try to derail our calling from God. This circle of accountability will push us forward instead of reinforcing undesired behaviors. The type of people you have closest to you currently is a strong indication of where you will be five years from now.

PROXIMITY MATTERS, AND BEING IN A CLOSE PROXIMITY WITH JESUS WILL STRONGLY INDICATE WHERE YOU ARE HEADED.

In our lives there are seasons of time we grow, develop, and are challenged because of a shepherd (mentor, leader) relationship that we have in our life. If you don't currently have these relationships in your life, reach out. Find a way to connect and get resources to develop areas in your life that you want and need to. If you are not shepherding/ mentoring anyone, reach out. You have much to offer someone, and people will benefit from learning about your journey. You have learned life lessons and gone through and won battles that need to be shared with others.

REFLECTION SECTION

WHAT IN YOUR LIFE HAS MADE YOU INSECURE?

_____

_____

_____

_____

WHAT DO YOU NEED TO NOT LET CONTROL YOUR DECISIONS AND ACTIONS?

_____

_____

_____

_____

NOTES:

_____

_____

_____

_____

4

WORK

This section may hurt some people's feelings and be really challenging to others, but oh, is this ever so important. Work can be such an ugly word or concept to some people. First hurt, here it comes: Work shouldn't be something that you have to do; it's what you get to do. It's all in your mindset. Even if you do not love what you are currently doing, you can do it with a joyful attitude and give it your best effort. If you approach it with frustration and "I have to do it," chances are it will not be a great day or week for you. For years I have watched people come and go from work with just the "I have to be here all day" tone in their voice and they can really kill the room. There is just this dark cloud that they create that is hard to get rid of. Nothing is worse than trying to get excitement going with Captain Buzz Kill hanging out in the room. I saw this demonstration once when someone took a big clear container and filled it

73

with plain water. This represented the normal "Let's go, everything's good" atmosphere. Here comes the negative. The person took just a few drops of black dye, and instantly, the container became cloudy and affected by the small, insignificant amount of dye introduced to the clear water. In turn, it takes an extremely large amount of water to flush out the effects of the black dye. The clean water that is poured into the container begins to help to return the water to completely clear but takes much more water than was originally in the container. It will start to overflow and replace the affected water, diluting the original container until it's clear.

People who lack joy or always act like nothing is good, everyone is terrible, and no one can do it right, have usually been the same way at the last seven jobs they have held or the churches they attended. I will not mention names, but I had a key associate once, and he could instantly change the room with his doom and gloom attitude. I gave him a silly nickname that quickly spread like wildfire through the entire team. Looking back, maybe that wasn't the most mature thing I could have done. Still, at the time, I was frustrated and was trying to help him see that things weren't that bad, and that it would work out. It would improve for him when he finally embraced the frustrations and attitude that was breaking up progress throughout the environment that we were a part of. It was a long time ago, and I have become a completely different person from back then. I would never handle someone's work ethic by a nickname and challenge a person in that way again. I just really struggled to find a way to motivate this guy. I could get him laughing and challenged him daily, but it was only temporary. That same guy, however, showed back up to work almost every day.

It may be a lot of work for some as we continue through the ways and obstacles of owning your purpose. It usually isn't easy; it's mostly a grind, but when you are in your purpose, you will know it, and the fulfillment you get from it will grow you and bring you so much joy. Work will develop behaviors and consistencies that you can take with you everywhere you go and will rub off on people around you as a shepherd would do!

Work is a biblical construct. The Bible starts with the story of God working. Genesis 2:2-3 says on the seventh day God had finished all His work of creating, so He took rest from working, blessing the seventh day and declaring it holy, because it was the day when He rested from all His work of creation. Think about the grass, mountains, oceans, everything in them, and humankind, all these came from God working. What an example of what we need to do. I mean, if God puts the work in, we need to live like Him, to take action and get to work. If you are capable of working, then get going.

After God created man, do you know what God told Adam to do? God didn't ask Adam to hang out, relax, and play video games, He gave him a purpose, an assignment, a job. God told Adam to name all the animals on the earth.

75

This could not have been some small feat, knowing how many animals and insects exist. It must have taken Adam a long time to name all these animals. I can't even imagine the process. Adam had to apply himself, owning his purpose, and began to work, naming the animals and insects. I can't imagine where names like hippopotamus and aardvark came from, but honestly, that's not my assignment to own.

Here is another example of someone who had to work in the Bible: Noah. Can you imagine being asked to build a giant boat because a colossal flood was coming to destroy the earth? God told Noah this was to protect his family and the animals He brought to Noah to save them from the flood. In Genesis 6, God gave Noah specific directions that he had to work at. The Ark was 300 cubits long, 50 cubits wide, and 30 cubits high. Cubits were the unit of measurement that was common at this time. The dimensions in feet are assumed to be 450' x 75' x 45'. This is a huge boat. The next boat to meet these dimensions would be the Titanic. The time estimated to grow and harvest the trees was around 60 years after God approached Noah to build the boat. It is thought it took 120 years to build the Ark. Talk about a workload. Noah lived a life of obedience, and through his respect for God and his purpose, he fulfilled his calling. Life would be utterly different if Noah perhaps chose his path and chose not to live out the purpose God gave him. Notice, though, his purpose was work; it took his commitment and effort to get it done.

Working can be defined as your personal applied efforts

towards accomplishing something, which then gives a specific desired set of results. Sounds simple and it really is. When you apply yourself to what you are trying to accomplish, things will get done. It doesn't always mean it's going to be perfect or even right, but something happens when you apply your effort; you begin to see the effects of work. Things start coming together, and you start getting the results you expected.

When you are owning your purpose, it is working towards a path God has paved for you, calling you to head into knowing that your purpose will require you to work and have partnership with God.

TRUSTING GOD AND OWNING YOUR PURPOSE WILL REQUIRE MUCH WORK, BLIND FAITH, AND FORWARD MOMENTUM.

You are trusting that the Lord knows what you need and that you have all that will be required of you already. Some of those skills are currently being developed or need to be developed.

Work only sometimes means that you are going to a job or that you get paid monetarily for the work you have done. Sometimes, work is also volunteering or serves a purpose or cause to benefit something or someone else. Maybe you set aside time to volunteer at your school to help set up for an event, or you volunteer your time for a clean-up day at a local organization that needs help but doesn't have the means to get it done. You can serve at a soup kitchen or a food drive to help those who are in need of food. At church, maybe you offer your assistance to help with ushering, greeting, the parking lot, and different ministries like nursery or children's church. In Colossians 3: 23-24, this is made pretty clear. "Whatever you do, do your work heartily, as for the Lord rather than for men, knowing that from the Lord you will receive the reward of the inheritance. It is the Lord Christ whom you serve." Serving and working as if you are serving Jesus directly puts work into such a different perspective. If you desire to be like Jesus, you will serve anyone. If you feel they don't deserve it, serve them anyway. Help them out, stretch yourself in every direction to be a blessing to someone. I can remember when my wife and I got married; she would always pull over by herself and give homeless people money. She was serving in a way she felt comfortable with. I looked at it like she was crazy. At the time I thought they don't deserve it, they are going to just buy alcohol or drugs, or waste it somehow. God has really spoken to me and showed me that I didn't deserve His grace either, but He gave it to me. I'm not the one that should be giving with a pre-thought of what they might do

78

with my gift; let God handle that. This could easily be the one act that changes their perspective on life and changes the direction that they are going.

Serving demonstrates that you sincerely care about someone or some cause. When you begin to serve regularly, it creates a feeling of joy because you are helping fulfil a need, expecting nothing in return. If you are serving with an expected blessing, then you are wasting your time. The blessing will come, but cannot be the reason you are helping someone. We are called to serve. Matthew 20:28 says, "just as the Son of Man did not come to be served, but to serve, and to give His life a ransom for many."

Who do we serve? How do we act this out? Who do you work for? If you feel called to the ministry, serve as pastor or in a church. If you feel called to own a restaurant, wash dishes for one, wait tables, offer to clean it up at the end of the night. If you want to be a farmer, offer to help bale hay for a season. All these things are going to take a good work ethic and dedication, but we have to extend ourselves all we can when we know that we are called to do so.

Work is such an integral part of our lifestyle and offers a sense of contentment when completing your projects, workday, volunteering, or tasks involving serving others. We cannot end this chapter without addressing one of the critical components of this equation. Working can be tiring and exhausting and really does deplete your body and spirit. We need to address the topic of rest. What??? Rest is important? Yes it is! Rest needs to be an integral part of your life for you to be successful in fulfilling your purpose. In the Bible, work is mentioned up to 400 times and rest 590 times, depending on the translation. It would seem like they both are super important to be said this many times, and need to be incorporated into our lives.

Rest provides so many benefits for you. It helps improve your mental health, boosts your immune system, reduces stress, and improves your attitude, all while improving your memory and concentration. Just that alone sounds great, but it also enhances our soul health. God shows us the importance of this right from the beginning in Genesis. Genesis chapter one explains what God does for six days and then in Genesis 2:2 it states, "By the seventh day God completed His work which He had done, and He rested on the seventh day from all His work which He had done." God took a break and rested from working. This must have been intentional, that the direction God gives from the beginning of His recorded story is work well and then relax. God creates the entire universe by speaking it into existence and then on the sixth day He paused to form man and woman. In Genesis 2:7 it says, "Then the Lord God formed man of dust from the ground and breathed into his nostrils the breath of life; and man became a living being." How beautiful that everything God did up to this point was spoken into existence, but then God took the time to form man in "our" image. Right from the beginning God said of the triune spirit, the three in one of God the Father, Son, and Holy Spirit. It wasn't just in His image, it was in Their image we were created. Everything written in the Bible is with specific intention. God is introducing what is coming later on.

Jesus shows us several examples of rest throughout the Gospels. Rest is about setting boundaries from what is keeping you moving; in Mark 4:35-39 Jesus was exhausted and fell asleep in the boat. A wild storm kicked up and the disciples began to panic, thinking they were about to die. Going to Jesus, they woke Him up; they were so worried about the storm they even asked Him if He cared if they died. Jesus got up and told the storm to be calm. The storm followed His order and just stopped. This is amazing to me; the disciples are seeing all sorts of miracles and still worried and had doubt because things were going wrong and they might not make it across. Then Jesus throws it out there, paraphrasing. "Do you still not have faith? Like really, guys? You don't realize that I got this?"

WHEN YOU ARE IN STORMS, JESUS HAS YOU; WHEN IT GETS SCARY AND WORSE THAN YOU EXPECTED, JESUS HAS YOU.

When you are living out your purpose, be aware that storms are coming; you will face obstacles that will challenge and stretch you. Know that Jesus will give you what you can handle with Him. It will be so challenging to perform your purpose without Him. This is an indicator that you are on the right path. Push forward. God will lead you if you are wandering off from your purpose.

Finally, work requires you to build a group or community of people that will encourage you and hold you accountable. You have to work at friendships and relationships for them to be successful and last. You have people who supervise or lead you at your place of work who are required to challenge or stretch you to be successful and creative with your given tasks and areas of responsibility. Work doesn't always need to be hard, but it will stretch and challenge you to be a better version of yourself. Let God work through you when building a better version of you. God will bless you for being focused on growing and representing yourself in the best way possible, a great steward of your time.

REFLECTION SECTION

WHAT DO YOU LIKE/DISLIKE ABOUT WORK?

_____

_____

_____

_____

DO YOU GIVE YOUR BEST EFFORTS AT WHAT YOU CURRENTLY DO?

_____

_____

_____

_____

NOTES:

_____

_____

_____

_____

_____

5

LIKE A PALM TREE

Strength, depending on the context in which the word is used, can mean many different things. It could mean you have a solid mental capacity to handle even the most challenging situations. You could be strong physically, meaning that you are healthy and can do a lot more than the average person. You can have a strong building, which means the construction is capable of withstanding weather and time. You can have strong stability, which means you don't shake easily, or you can have a strong smell, meaning you stink. I had to put that in here. It's funny how one adjective can be used in so many ways.

Let's talk about a bodybuilder who is concerned with their strength and is focused on the amount of weight they can lift, the size of the muscles they have, and the conditioning it takes to develop the strength behind the muscles and physique they have. Muscles are strengthened by the constant breaking down and building up they go through. As muscles are worked, they are stretched and broken down to only be built up more muscular for the next workout. Over time, muscles get stronger and stronger the more they are stretched and broken down. It's unlikely that you can walk up to 300 lbs. of weight on the bar at the weight bench and lift it the first time with no training and no conditioning. Don't think you can simply lift it off the rack, complete a full bench press, and put it back with little effort. You will probably struggle and strain until you want to give up. It would be best if you built a foundation that allows you to achieve what you are trying to accomplish by conditioning your body. Without the proper conditioning, you will struggle to achieve the goals that you have for yourself.

It's the same process when strengthening your mental game. The more positive you take in, the better you can put good out into the world. If you want to improve your knowledge capacity, reading more allows you to know more; studying more will enable you to be ready for the test easier. You can't take the test without ever being introduced to the subject. You have to develop and build your brain with the info that you need to obtain to grow in what you know. I don't know if you have ever been introduced to calculus, but if you are exposed to it for the first time the likelihood that you will be able to explain or solve what is going on is unlikely. I started college at 17 and went right into taking calculus. When I took the college entrance exams at 16, they said I was ready for calculus. I said sure, but I had no idea what I was getting into. See, high school was easy for me and I really didn't have to try hard to do well, which was not at all what college was like. So, I was completely unprepared for the class. I didn't study, barely did the homework, and I ended up getting a D for calculus one and then took calculus two and got an F. Embarrassing hardly sums up how I felt about my performance; it was like I was standing at that weight bench ready to go for 300 lbs. and barely able to lift the bar. My first year of college I was not strengthening my brain at all. I had too much freedom and missed classes, and I made a mess for myself. I got a letter stating that I was on the academic probation list and I had this semester to get it together or I was out of school. A 1.3 GPA is an accomplishment. However, the second year was different, very different. I humbled myself and retook both calculus 1 and 2, this time asking questions, doing extra work, and getting a B and an A respectively. It definitely cost me a lot because of my lack of training and conditioning to fulfill my expected and desired results. I ended up with a 3.8 GPA overall because I realized I had to apply myself to get it together.

If you want to learn more, you work at it. You have to stretch your current abilities by adding to what knowledge you currently have. If you're going to learn for school or college, then you have to work at it. You have to apply yourself and strengthen your mind to make it happen. If you want to be well-versed in God, then you have to know the Bible and apply what you are learning. If you want to learn what God has for you, then start by reading the Bible. It's the best way that we can learn from God, hear from him, and be changed from Him. It sounds funny, but the Bible will read you and give you what you need. God will use it to strengthen and grow you.

In the construction of anything, the strength and stability of the building comes from the design and strength of the foundation. A foundation is what sort of structure something is built upon. Whether we are talking about concrete, solid ground, rules, tenets, or principles, we need a solid start to build upon and grow.

I know this chapter is called "Like a Palm Tree." I promise I will get to that soon. But understanding the foundations of just about anything will make so much more sense when we get to the trees.

Foundations are determined by the need and requirements of what you are building. The environment determines the need for the depth of the footers, the materials needed in the construction matter where you are building. When you are building a home and go with the cheapest builder, it may look impressive at first, but when shortcuts are taken in making the foundation, eventually the structure will become compromised and begin to fail. When it begins to fail, it could be slow, a little at a time, or tragically all at once. The entire structure can be lost due to a shortcut in the decisions made around building the foundation, the main part of the building that you don't often look at, or easily take for granted, because you don't usually think or care about what you don't look at or see often. So much goes into building a foundation. It takes a plan that is engineered by experts who know what the requirements are so it won't fail.

Building a good, strong foundation is often very complex and challenging. You need to be well versed in the type of building, the size of the building, kind of structure, the design, framing, wood or metal materials. All of this will determine the type of foundation it will require. You don't need a skyscraper foundation for a stick building. Or you can't build a house in a swamp without a modified style of foundation. For example, the majority of buildings in Amsterdam in the Netherlands were built on the water. They used large wooden poles that they would push down through the water and into the soil till they reached a solid, strong layer of dry ground that wouldn't move. Then they built a stone foundation on this so it could support the buildings. Without the stilts in Amsterdam, that city would not be there today unless it was all made out of boats.

Spiritually, your foundation in Christ needs to be built in a similar way. Your strength through Christ needs to be made using the right tools to last through any storm you face. Nothing can win against you when you have God in your corner. The formula for building the proper foundation is prayer, reading your Bible, and worship, which are all fundamental building blocks of your foundation in Christ. It would be best if you also had a strong community of people that will speak life into you and that you can lean on when you are weak or feeling weathered by the storms you are currently in.

Palm trees are amazing. To start with, they are not trees. They are part of the grass family. They were created in such a way that when faced with storms and are stretched. This causes the palm to become stronger through the stretching. The palm tree's root system is strong, and they are often challenged when battled in a storm, with winds up to 140 mph. They are created in such a way that they bend and stretch when faced with adversity. The bending and stretching are unique, because they don't just go back to normal, they grow into the stretch and increase the length of the roots and the amount of ground they can hold onto, which makes them even more efficient when it comes to the next storm. Sounds a lot like a bodybuilder. The more work that is put in and the more challenges that the muscles face, the more likely they can be prepared to lift the new weight and face more complicated challenges. Like your body's muscles, palm trees grow stronger through the stretching and the storms they are faced with. We can grow in the same way.

THE MORE WE SEEK GOD, THE MORE PREPARED WE CAN BE TO MAKE IT THROUGH THE CHALLENGING SEASONS AND TO GROW INTO OUR PURPOSE.

Each storm will be difficult and complex; it teaches us to have faith, trust in God, and learn the purpose of the storm we face.

A palm tree's chance of survival is 40-50% more when planted with other palms like itself. When planted in groups, the roots can work together and increase their strength and how much of a storm's wrath they can handle. We are wired the same way; belonging to a group of like-minded people with a common focus and similar goals will give you a support structure that builds your strength and that of others as well. Your ability to get through your challenging seasons or difficult times increases when you have a group of people to call to and lean on. Someone else's strength and faith can lift your faith so you can get your feet under you. They can pray for you, encourage you, meet with you, and help establish reliable roots within your foundation for what you face next time. The palm branch is a symbol of life, as in the original Palm Sunday, for starters. Christians would often carry palm branches around to symbolize when Jesus came into Jerusalem, fulfilling a prophecy foretold by Zechariah. It was said that people cut the palm branches from the trees and laid them on the street when Jesus entered the city. This is written about in the gospels of Luke 19, John 12, and Matthew 21. The palm branch symbolizes victory, triumph, peace, and eternal life. Palm trees, also known as tamar in Hebrew, are mentioned in the Bible in Exodus 15:27: "They came into Elim, where there were twelve springs of water and seventy palm trees: and so, they encamped there by the water." They found refuge amongst the palms and water. Palms are mentioned at least 30 times throughout the Bible. The strength of the palm comes from the development of its foundation. Your ability to own your purpose will come as you develop your foundation. They are strengthening through trials and learning to lean on God through tough seasons. Developing great habits and routines will aid in increasing the strength of your foundation.

Pure strength comes from God when you trust in Him. The Bible clearly lays it out amongst the pages from cover to cover. Strength is mentioned over 360 times in the Bible, including both natural and supernatural strength. We need both kinds to be able to live out our purpose successfully. Thessalonians 5:11 says, "Therefore encourage one another and build each other up, just as you are doing." Just like palm trees, our strength is increased when we have those around us to lean on. Even when you don't feel like you've got it all together or don't feel strong, don't give up; endure.

GOD WILL GIVE YOU ALL THE STRENGTH YOU NEED WHEN YOU HAVE A SOLID RELATIONSHIP WITH HIM.

Get into the Bible, and it will guide you as God will use it to speak to you.

Psalm 121:1-2 says, "I lift up my eyes to the mountains; where does my help come from? My help comes from the Lord, the maker of heaven and earth." You have to choose to pursue your relationship with God. You get to acknowledge that your strength comes from Him, and He will allow you to follow Him and your purpose.

Isaiah 41:10, "So do not fear, for I am with you; do not be dismayed, for I am your God, I will strengthen you and help you; I will uphold you with my righteous right hand." Don't give up. Stay focused, keep your eyes on Jesus, and trust that He assigns your purpose. Your purpose will not always be something that you had any idea that you had in you or something that you wanted to do. Jesus will give you strength when you lean on Him. Your purpose will be uniquely yours, that you and only you can fulfill as God intended. We all need people in our corner to give us strength in the tough times, when we feel weak—the extra support to make it through any storm. We are stronger with God in our corner and a support group of a select few that will encourage us and keep us moving forward and planted no matter what we are facing.

Do you have friends that strengthen you when you need it? It's so vital to have someone to lean on, a group of people that will tell you the truth and not hold back. They will pick you up when you fall and clean the stones from your knees when you do.

Are you that support for someone? Are you reaching out to those when you feel the prompting?

Are you sending a random text to those you think about? It might be the exact strength they need in that moment, a moment of encouragement that you can offer someone who needs it. Develop that tight root system with a group where you all help each other grow and support each other when one is in trouble.

LIKE A PALM TREE

REFLECTION SECTION

DO YOU HAVE RELATIONSHIPS THAT STRENGTHEN YOU IN YOUR LIFE?

_____

_____

_____

_____

_____

_____

NOTES:

_____

_____

_____

_____

_____

_____

_____

6

ANTICIPATION AND REACTIONS

Simply living daily life will be complicated. It's full of obstacles and events that can derail us at any time and any turn that we make, but we have a choice. Anything can come our way, and our choices can take us out of the way or put us directly into the path of getting hit by it all. We can live out a life driven by purpose or react to all events that come to us. If you look at several different sports, they are all played with anticipation and reactions. Reactions are necessary, but when a good plan is in play using anticipation and routines, you have the space and ability to react more efficiently.

Let's look at some different sports to understand anticipation. In baseball, the pitcher and catcher have a relationship that has to be built on trust and anticipation.

The catcher tells the pitcher what to throw, and when agreed upon, the catcher knows the position to be in to anticipate the pitch. They have prepared plans and communication to understand what they are going to do. If the catcher asks for a curveball and the pitcher agrees and then throws a fast ball, they are putting themselves in a possible spot to miss the throw or give up a hit to the other team. The field players have a better chance at the play when the pitcher and catcher have excellent communication and execute well.

Basketball, soccer, and hockey are all similar, with well executed plays that the team practices over and over again to be able to anticipate each other's moves. Every player has to be in their designated spot to accomplish what was well planned and practiced, to anticipate that on this specific spot, they make a play and that the other players are just in their spot and ready to go. It's terrific when the players don't even have to double-check each other because the other players are anticipating the play and are doing their part.

Being purposeful in your steps allows your reactions to be meaningful. If an opponent is right where you need to be, then you have to react accordingly.

Like sports, living a life of anticipation is so critical to living a balanced life so that you can maximize your time, resources, and energy. Just as important as living life to the fullest, you plan out the time to work, have fun, and, most importantly, rest.

Exodus 20:8-1 states, "Remember the sabbath day, to keep it holy. Six days you shall labor and do all your work, but the seventh day is a sabbath of the Lord your God; in it, you shall not do any work, you or your son or your daughter, your male or your female servant or your cattle or your sojourner who stays with you." God told us to rest, relax, stop working, and recharge just one of the seven days a week.

This is living in anticipation, making a plan, and executing it. If you know you currently have no plans for two days, what are you going to do? What are you anticipating for your day off? Are there going to be things you have to say no to? Even if you don't want to say no, it's the only effective way to fulfill and live in your purpose.

Let me give you an example. I love mowing the lawn. It's time for me to relax, think, enjoy the sun, and spend time with God. It's the repetition of going back and forth repeatedly that is satisfying to me. So, for me, lawn mowing is not work. However, weed trimming or landscaping is so tedious to me and feels like work to me, so that happens on a day when I'm already working. See, what is work to me might not be work for you. You might enjoy painting and it's relaxing to you but for me, no way. It's work.

In a faith sense, living in anticipation is not waiting around; it's getting ready or completing what God told you to do. I'll show you here in Hebrews 11:7. "By faith

Noah, being warned by God about things not yet seen, in reverence prepared an ark for the salvation of his household, by which he condemned the world, and became an heir of the righteousness which is according to faith."

In Genesis 6-7, we read of the fall of mankind and the flood. Noah found favor among the people around him, and God told him that he would be spared and not punished as the rest of the world was about to be. God gave Noah specific measurements and expectations of how the boat should be planned and constructed. How many floors, where the windows went, even where the door should be.

Genesis 6:22, "Thus Noah did; according to all that God had commanded him, so he did." Noah set out in anticipation to complete his purpose. To save two of every animal and his wife, sons, and their wives. Living in anticipation, God still gives you a choice. Today would be very different if Noah made different choices. Noah saw the importance of the favor God shown on his life.

You are always young enough to live in your purpose. Noah built this boat when he was over 500 years old; it says that the floods came when Noah was 600 years old. I can't imagine being alive in my 600's, let alone tackling what Noah was being called to do, but completing your task when you are called to do so takes a choice and desire to want to do what you are called to do. The task alone of building the boat, planting all the trees, only anticipating that he would need to cut them down to make a boat to prepare for something he had no idea what it would be or what it was going to look like, other than trusting that God gave him all the info that he needed to complete the task. A flood was coming that would completely change all he and his family knew, which would set a new path for himself and his family to reset the world as it was once known. This is a great demonstration of what purpose is and how it is placed in front of us. Look at the blueprints for the boat God designed. He knew it would need rooms and a specific length and height to hold all He called Noah to collect. Noah wasn't just collecting the animals he liked, he collected all of them and did was expected of him.

YOUR PURPOSE REQUIRES ALL OF YOU AND ALL OF YOUR COMMITMENT, NOT JUST THE PARTS THAT YOU CHOOSE TO SURRENDER OR THE PARTS THAT YOU ARE WILLING TO LET GOD USE.

It takes a full commitment in anticipation to know that God has it, and when we walk towards the calling, God will reveal and direct our steps when we get to where we are going.

When I was three or four, I remember being told that my biological father was coming to take me on an ice fishing trip. I devoured breakfast, and my grandmother got me dressed and put my coat on me, getting me all bundled up so I was ready to go. I can honestly remember wearing my tan corduroy pants, a long-sleeved navy shirt, and snow boots. I was anticipating his arrival, waiting for the moment he pulled into the driveway to take me ice fishing. Fishing is still one of my favorite things to do. I waited what felt like hours (I really don't know how long it was, but it was forever), sitting at the top of the large wooden staircase with a patterned carpet runner all the way down it. As I slowly made my way down the staircase, I took my coat off and my gloves and then my boots and sat on the old stairs, wondering what I did to be left behind, forgotten about in that moment. Why was I not important enough to be picked up and taken on a fishing trip? God doesn't work like this. God will be here for you in all the moments. When you feel that you don't have it all together and it looks bleak, know your Father in Heaven is here, present with you all the time, during all the moments, whether you think so or not.

See, as a kid I didn't understand the circumstances around him not being present and I know that I carried those insecurities of abandonment around with me for years. I didn't understand why he wasn't around or the events that led to his departure, but I am now able to realize that people will always let you down. People are not perfect and will always struggle to be consistent 100% of the time. They cannot do it right every time, and that is hard for us to grasp. They are not wired to be perfect. We can always strive to be the best for everyone, but it will not happen. We will always fall short of perfection.

Living your life in anticipation for tomorrow is good, but you cannot forget to enjoy the journey and live in the moment. Sometimes I find myself constantly looking forward to what is next so it's hard to remember I need to enjoy the present as well. When I was in grade school it would be Monday morning and I was like, "We've only got four days left." The week had barely even begun, and I was already anticipating its ending. "It is Wednesday, now we've only got two days left." Later it changed to, "I'm going to be 16 soon, I'm getting my car soon, I cannot wait." I didn't know that my excitement at getting my first car would come with all sorts of extra costs like oil changes, gas, new tires, brakes, and car insurance. What a pain all that is; I was not ready for all that extra for my $500 car. It was a Renault Alliance and in okay shape. I couldn't put more than a half a tank of gas in it or it would leak. What was an even cooler feature was in the winter on frigid days when you opened the door the locking mechanism would stay frozen and would not latch for a good 20 minutes or so. This car was also a manual five speed so I would have to shift in between holding the door closed and trying to prevent it from swinging open while I was driving around. I can laugh now, but it was not funny at all back then. I was even driving around long enough so that the door would warm up enough to be able to lock the car.

Living in anticipation of tomorrow will only sometimes work out the way you hope. We need to live the moments we get and enjoy the journey we are on so we can fulfill the purpose and promise God has put on our hearts when the time arrives. We have to always keep moving forward; we cannot just wait for life to come to us. It will never reach where we need it to be if we sit around and make no choices about what comes our way.

Our choices are our reactions to what we think we need to do. Noah had to respond within what he was anticipating. He had to cut the trees and shape them into the pieces he needed. He had to form the pieces into the shape of the boat that God had explained to him, what it was and how it needed to look. God is in our anticipations and our reactions, and these are both needed to head in the direction He has called us to go. The key to all of this is that God is in it. He is with you, and all the decisions that you make will go so much better when He is with you in your decision-making process. Don't attempt to live out your given purpose without including God. It will feel empty and lonely, and it will lack joy.

REFLECTION SECTION

WHAT ARE THINGS IN YOUR LIFE
THAT YOU ARE REACTING TO THAT
WITH A PLAN IT WOULD WORK OUT
MUCH BETTER?

_____

_____

_____

_____

WHAT ARE THINGS YOU CAN
ANTICIPATE IN YOUR FUTURE?

_____

_____

_____

_____

NOTES:

_____

_____

_____

_____

7

WHY NOT ME?

Growing up, if I made money, I spent it. If it was in my possession, I would blow it. I worked for the family flooring business during the summer when I was young. I would assist my grandfather in cleaning job sites and loading and unloading the work vehicles. I would install some flooring when he trusted me to do it. Most of the time I would install the subfloors or clean the tiles after they were grouted. It was fun spending most days with him and learning so much about flooring installation and building whatever needed to be done. My dad did the accounting for the business, and when it was time to write the paychecks every week, my dad would hold back an extra percentage so I would have a surprise check at the end of the summer. This money was for school clothes, a trip to an amusement park, or something fun. With my dad knowing me and the way I was always chasing whatever everyone else had, he knew I would spend it all and have nothing by the end of the weekend. I was mad at first when I found out that I was "going without" during the summer because I was horrible with money and didn't even realize it. It took me awhile to realize that my dad was giving me what I could barely handle and I wasn't ready for more, because I had learned nothing at that point. God works with us in the same way. He doesn't give us more than we can handle without Him. If you can steward it well, it will come. Paul writes in 1 Corinthians 10:13, "No temptation has overtaken you but such as is common to man; and God is faithful, who will not allow you to be tempted beyond what you are able, but with the temptation will provide the way of escape also, so that you will be able to endure it."

God will never give you more than you and God can handle together. You will struggle with your purpose if you try to live it without Him, making decisions that benefit you and not the plan. You will make it hard on yourself. A decision that takes a different than intended plan will only lead to a longer, different path to the destination. Going through the valleys is crucial to developing and growing in your purpose. If you are taking the bridges all along to skip the valleys, you will not have developed the skillset required for your purpose, God's plan for your life.

CHASING WHAT EVERYONE ELSE HAS WILL ONLY DELAY WHAT GOD HAS FOR YOU.

You have to give up your agenda and die to your own plans to fulfill God's will for your life. It is funny how it works, though; God will give you the desires of your heart, or your heart will change as you surrender yourself to God's will.

Do you ever wonder why everyone else seems to be getting theirs, and it just doesn't happen for you? In Psalms 73:1-3 Asaph writes: "Surely God is good to Israel, to those who are pure in heart! But as for me, my feet came close to stumbling; my steps had almost slipped. For I was envious of the arrogant As I saw the prosperity of the wicked." Asaph is so concerned with wicked people prospering, and he is good and is struggling. His envy and jealousy almost take him out. Do you look at others and want what they have? Do you wish you had as nice a car or house as them? Do you wish that you could wear the same clothes as them? The problem with jealousy is that it will take you out, always hoping for what you don't have. When you live a life with your purpose, you will have all you need. It's hard to grasp why someone else is having a ball, and you can barely make it paycheck to paycheck. God gives us what we can handle with His help and guidance. If you are listening to God and doing as He directs, then you might not be able to be trusted with more. We must be good stewards of what we have before we will likely be entrusted with more. Jealousy will always lead you down a road of forever disappointment and you will never be satisfied with what you have, because you are constantly chasing the next thing.

I used to put so much value on what clothing I wore and what I owned. Being taller than most kids in my class, I always felt that I stuck out, and it was apparent that I wasn't wearing the name-brand clothes and shoes that everyone else was. If I wasn't wearing name-brand jeans or sneakers, I didn't even want to be seen. I was already dealing with insecurities about who I was. I thought that if I dressed the part, maybe the person I felt like wouldn't show up, just the facade I was making up for everyone to see and get to know. I was always bummed that I never got the newest sneakers, the latest Walkman, mp3 players, or the newest game system that just came out. Why was it that my family couldn't get me what I wanted, like everyone else had? Why not me? Why did we not have all the cool stuff I desired? This is why the feeling I carried has shown up in my life all along since I was young. I always had to have the most CDs, DVDs, clothes, whatever it was that I had to have; I would overindulge; excess was what I defined as how I would do everything. My parents did the best they could with what they had, but I could only see that once I was older. They would often get us clothes for birthdays and Christmas as well as some toys and fun stuff. Christmas was always so much fun, but being humble here, I was always a bit disappointed. It wasn't that my parents didn't give so much; I was always wanting what everyone else got. I have changed so much now, but it was always: why not me?

We all do this at different times in our lives. I will share some examples of things I went through. School gym class team picking was the worst. Someone always got picked without even thinking about it. Sometimes I got picked early but other times I would get picked towards the end. Nothing was worse than being the last one standing and being told you are on team B, like no one liked you but by default you are going to that team. In your head, you would be saying things like, "Why am I picked last? Why don't they like me? They don't even know that I'm pretty good at sports." I remember one gym class game of softball; I was picked towards the very end. I was up to bat, and the outfield players came into the baseline thinking I would have no game in me at all. I swung at that ball so hard and missed that it turned me around entirely in the other direction. However, the second pitch was much different. I sent that ball to the outfield fence, scoring a few runs for my team and getting to third base. The rush of excitement I had in me fueled me for the rest of the game. My next up at bat, the gym teacher told them to back up this time. Knowing things with me were not as they seemed, things for gym class started to change for me. I wasn't getting picked last anymore, but I was always concerned that I would be able to show up and perform each and every game.

When it came to work, I remember asking myself "Why not me?" so many times. I was always trying to do the best job I could at whatever I did. I remember getting called into work once when we were enjoying a summer vacation at a rented cottage on Lake Ontario. My dad asked who was on the phone; I told him my work called to see if I could work that evening. I told them I was out of town, so I wasn't available. He made me call them back and tell them I would be there in 30 minutes. He made it very clear that if work calls you go; if they choose you, you go. I still live with this ethic today, but did it frustrate me in that moment. Oh yes, it did! I kept asking myself, "Why can't I enjoy time off? Why do I have to go to work?" He showed me the opposite perspective on this, for sure. Why not me? I was choosing to accept my narrow perspective. They picked me because they thought I would be reliable and come through when they needed someone—that moment changed so much for me at work. I'm glad my dad took time to show me the objective perspective instead of my narrow, frustrated, selfish view. My selfish views followed me deep into my career and really put my relationships, including my marriage, into some challenging times. I put work first in almost every area of my life. It should have been, God first, my wife second, then our kids, but that's not how I saw things. It was work first, then Jeremy, and then everything else. I can remember getting home from traveling for ten days and sitting on the couch answering the dozens of emails I needed to respond to for work and then off to the motocross track to ride on my day off. Why not me? I took that to the extreme and it was always about me, because I ensured it was. I never took anything to God, felt empty and alone even though I had so much. My whole identity was formed by what I had achieved, how hard I worked, and what my employees or boss thought of me. My son Noah finally helped me see what my wife Stephanie had been trying to help me see all along. He asked me, "Dad, when do you go back home?" I was home, did he really think I didn't live here? I was confused and broken. I was so focused on what I had to be that I forgot totally about what was necessary. I was everything I needed to be for the company, but I couldn't even see that my wife and kids were looking for me to be present, to be a husband, and to be home. The only title that my children cared about was "Dad." The fact that I was gone enough for my children to question if I even lived with them was an eye-opening experience, especially when you pause and ask, "Why not me?"

"WHY NOT ME?" HAPPENS WHEN YOU ARE CHASING SOMETHING THAT MIGHT NOT BE FOR YOU.

It might be something that you are wasting your time on, pursuing what was never intended for you, because you were focused on your benefit and not God's will. You might be pursuing what God has for you in the wrong season, and if you are not ready for it, it will not fit easily into your schedule and timing. When the timing is right, God will help you make a way. Please find the time and access to fulfill what He is looking for in your life. When you give in to God's will, it provides you the capacity for so much more. You will begin to find time for your passions when you put Him first.

Jealousy and envy will consume you when you forget to enjoy all that you have. When you look at someone who always seems to have something new and exciting, the urge that you have to have it as well takes over. You think deserve it. "Why not me?" wins. Jealousy robs you of any joy you can experience, and then frustration and sadness take over because you want what they have. When you own your purpose, you will embrace what you have because it is all you need. This doesn't mean that you go through life without buying things that you will enjoy and have fun with. These things have to fit within the context of your life and the means that you have to acquire them. I really want a Bentley Bentayga. This SUV is so nice. I will keep enjoying the pictures I find, because it doesn't fit into our life right now. This doesn't mean I can't want one; it just means that the time and means to acquire it are just not available right now. Someday I might own one, but when and if it is time, I will so enjoy it. With this said, any time someone gets a new vehicle I get excited for them; I congratulate them and celebrate with them that they could get one.

Romans 12:9-10 NLT states, "Don't just pretend to love others. Really love them. Hate what is wrong. Hold tightly to what is good. Love each other with genuine affection, and take delight in honoring each other." Give to others, even if they don't need it or deserve it. God calls us to love each other. Suppose you find yourself starting to feel jealous about what someone else has or received. Celebrate them. There is no better way to beat jealousy than to go head-on with what is attempting to overtake you. Deny the urge to covet what they have and be excited for what you have.

If someone gets a brand-new car, be happy for them. When someone gets a promotion and you did not, celebrate with them. God will provide for you when it's the right time and He will fulfill your needs. Why not me? It is you when your perspective develops and changes for the season you're in.

REFLECTION SECTION

WHAT DO YOU FEEL ABOUT THE QUESTION, WHY NOT ME?

_____

_____

_____

_____

WHAT AREAS DO YOU COMPARE YOURSELF TO OTHERS?

_____

_____

_____

_____

NOTES:

_____

_____

_____

_____

8

WHAT IF I HAVE IT ALL WRONG? PASSION AND PURPOSE

Have you ever spent the whole night studying for the biggest test of the year only to realize that you have spent all the time preparing for the test, studying the wrong chapter? So frustrated and annoyed that you wasted so much time focused on the wrong thing only you are not really ready for the test. I have been there and experienced that. Yes, you are not prepared for what you should have been ready for, but you learned something that you hadn't known before. You are prepared, just for the wrong test or thing. Life can be like this often. You spend so much time focused on one thing only to realize that you are supposed to be headed in another direction. Your timing was wrong, so you might have spent money you didn't need to, or you might have to redirect your focus to learn what you should've prepared for, but it now takes time from something else. Like the studying you did set you up for something later on that you will face; you just learned it when you needed to focus on something else.

Your purpose will define you and fulfill you better than anything.

THERE ARE NO PROCESSES OR POSSESSIONS THAT WILL FILL YOU WITH MORE CONTENTMENT THAN LIVING OUT YOUR PURPOSE.

Material things will give you momentary joy, but it will wear off. It's a joy like caffeine. You get some energy and revived feeling and then comes the crash. There is a reason why so many people run to coffee when their feet touch the floor getting out of bed. It gives you that momentary hit of contentment until it doesn't. It starts off making you feel good and gets you going in a good direction and then boom, you start falling off in the intensity that you had moments ago. The path of purpose is not a straight line. There are no cheat codes or paved paths with street signs everywhere saying, "Go this way." You almost have it; you are so close, only a couple of turns left. There is no GPS device for this purpose. You have to seek to understand what you are here for and how you are going to go after it.

When you begin to worry if you have it all wrong, do you take the time to evaluate if you are focused on what you want, or what God has for you? This is the conversation around passion vs. purpose. Passion begins with what you want to do or experience, things that you love or enjoy doing. Passion is defined as an intense desire or enthusiasm for something. I have spent most of my life chasing my passions. I didn't understand that God had a purpose for me, or that purpose was something that we all had, until a few years ago. For many years, I went all in with BMX; I spent several summers at Woodward Sports Camp for extreme sports. I went to events everywhere, subscribed to every BMX magazine available starting "pre-internet." I would travel all over to ride at different parks. I started riding BMX, then discovered the wheelie, and jumps came right after. I took several years away due to finances and opportunities. I started riding again in the late 90s and until 2010, I was all in; it quickly became the one thing I gave my all to, and it consumed so much of my time and money. It was so much fun, traveling and riding, whether it was in skateparks or street riding. Street riding uses obstacles like parking barriers, curbs, railings, ledges, etc. You learn a lot about balance and become creative when it's not just a ramp made for riding. I met a lot of cool people, several police officers, and had some mad and crazy people chasing me as well. I have broken so many bones and had a couple of concussions, causing a couple of small scars on my brain throughout this long season in my life. I wanted so badly to get the ability to become a professional rider, to be known in the sport, but with the knee surgery and all the issues that happened, the sport just progressed so fast away from me. I started riding motorcycles, which led to motocross as well. Hey, if I couldn't pedal up a ramp, I was going to give a pull on a throttle to see if I could make it happen. Of course, I went all in. Rode several different motocross bikes and traveled to ride at several different moto parks to see if I could get the hang of it and make it to a place where I could be competitive. I chased full speed, getting all the gear and memberships I needed to join the sport. Biking is simply in my blood; the adrenaline is so much fun. It pushes you to go bigger and faster when everything goes the way it should. I had so much fun, but none of this fun ever seemed to fulfill a need in my soul. There has always been something missing. I spent so much time dedicated to fulfilling my need to stay busy and consume and learn everything I could about the sport. It's not wasted time from my life; I just had the priorities in my life all over the place. I had no relationship with God, and learning about God and my purpose was completely not part of my plan. I used to love fishing when I was a young kid and spent

120

every day I could fishing, from sunup to sundown during school vacation. It was always so much fun for me. I was so hyper and always had to be in motion; I could barely ever sit still and was always going what seemed like 100 mph, but fishing somehow would be an outlet for me to sit all day long and just try to figure out how to get the fish to bite. With all my injuries, I stopped riding bikes as much and started fishing more and more. Soon, fishing gave me the same fulfillment that BMX and motorcycles once had. It gave me hope that I could make a name for myself, be a professional, and possibly excel in fishing tournaments and the sport. My priority was my passion. It was all about me. I was hoping that my passions would fulfill something I needed. Now, I would love someday to make it into tournament fishing, but I am no longer chasing my passion as a priority. I still really enjoy fishing; I just no longer put it first. If God makes a way that I can fish as a professional angler that would be amazing and I will give it everything I can, but if it doesn't happen that's okay as well. When I go fishing, I always treat it with the mindset that I'm preparing for a tournament. I work to break down the lake bottom, fish patterns, water current, and water temperature to make wise decisions about where the bass should be. Sometimes I do great and other times I don't quite figure out what is happening.

For so many years, I spent so much of my focus and time chasing my life's passions and always wondered why it never quite worked out. It's honestly simple, looking back now. Proverbs 3:6 NLT says, in everything you do, put God first, and he will direct you and crown your efforts with success. I was not doing this. God came after everything in my life. I had it all backwards. It wasn't until the last five years that I started to reverse the order of importance in my life. When I fish now, God is always in it. If I go by myself, I spend a lot of time talking to God and just conversing with Him. If I'm fishing with a friend, we have a great time talking and enjoying the day. However, now I know God is always with me. If you put God first in your life, He makes room for your passions. Your passions adapt more and more when you have God front and center in your life. Your priorities become more focused on what God wants when you spend more time with Him. Passions are important to have. They give you something to focus your energy and time on. They might be a way to express your talents and give you joy, but they can't be your priority.

WHEN YOUR FIRST PASSION BECOMES JESUS AND SEEKING HIM, IT CHANGES EVERYTHING.

Matthew 6:32-33 NLT says, "These things dominate the thoughts of unbelievers, but your heavenly Father already knows your needs. Seek the Kingdom of God above all else, and live righteously, and he will give you everything you need." You will have time for your passions when you express your first commitment to God's purpose for your life. Often people will have it wrong when it comes to owning their purpose, because they forget the one thing that will lead them in the right direction. They forget to seek God. When you seek God earnestly, He will help you see where you are going. When you see your purpose, you will see where you are going but not the destination or maybe you know where you are supposed to end up but have no idea of the path to get there. This is where faith kicks in and boom, you start. James 2:26 says that just as the body without the spirit is dead, so also faith without works is dead.

Passions are remarkable and can bring you immense joy when they are not what you are trying to find fulfillment from. Whether it was two-wheeled action sports or fishing, they both gave me so much joy but never gave me all I needed. The joy was limited, lacking something I was searching for. It was like an energy drink; it gives you energy for a moment, but then you quickly crash and become empty again. In extreme sports, a backflip on a motorcycle is a massive stunt. It was considered a holy grail of tricks., thought to be impossible. In 2015, one man set out to try and take this to another level by attempting and landing a triple back flip on a motocross bike. Unbelievably, it was only a few years before that the backflip was thought to be unachievable in a motored sport. Passions are much the same as chasing the impossible in extreme sports. Once you get whatever out of your passion you are seeking, you begin to add something else to take it further. You will never be content. Don't get me wrong. Progression is excellent and necessary in sports and to develop new skillsets. I set out to learn something new every day, but this will never be the "thing" that will complete you like seeking God and to own your purpose.

Purpose is what we are called to do. It is the space God has designated us for, that only we can fulfill as God intended. When you surrender to God and are focused on what God wants you to do, things start to happen that are designed for the time you are in.

YOUR PURPOSE WILL TAKE YOU OUT OF YOUR COMFORT ZONE AND STRETCH YOU, CHALLENGE YOU, AND PUT YOU IN A POSITION WHERE YOU NEED TO REACH OUT TO HIM FOR GUIDANCE AND INSTRUCTION.

It's honestly hard to comprehend that your plan and mine was written long before we were born; it was orchestrated perfectly long ago. Esther 4:14 says, "For if you remain silent at this time, relief and deliverance will arise for the Jews from another place and you and your father's house will perish. And who knows whether you have not attained royalty for such a time as this?" You are called to where you are now to fulfill what only you can, here and now.

What are you doing? What distractions are keeping you from your purpose? What are you waiting for? Do you feel disqualified? I have been broken and messed up most of my life. If God is still willing to use me, then you have no excuse. Are you choosing your passions over choosing to ask God, "What am I here for? What do You want for me? What in this life can I possibly be here for?"

You can start seeking God for your purpose today. Ask yourself questions like: "Can I do this on my own? I think I know my purpose and it is so easy, can this be it? I can't do what I think I'm supposed to do because no one will understand." This is a really hard one, because parents and grandparents want what is best for their children and if they are not seeking God for your calling on your life, they too can get in the way of God's will. Now, my grandparents always spoke life into me, and they always talked to me about being in the ministry. I had no intentions of taking them seriously, yet here I am, beginning to spend time working in the ministry. I think God gave them a preview that I just wasn't ready to accept or listen to back then.

Even though they have been gone for years now, thank God for grandparents who prayed for all of their family. Their prayers are still being answered today. It's amazing what God releases in your life in the right season and the right place, and what and who God places in your path to encourage you and develop what you need in your life. I had nothing to do with selecting my grandparents, but God did. The phrase "But God" will come up constantly when you are in your purpose. "But God" can only be understood as something wouldn't have happened without God; it wouldn't be possible because it seems impossible, but somehow it happened. Somehow God made a way where there is no road yet; we still got there. Living in your purpose and owning it will transform the operation of your life. What your life becomes through your obedience and striving to learn and live God's will for you opens doors. Purposeful living in God's will changes the ceiling of your life. God will expand your reach as you prove to be trusted with what He has already given you. Your purpose expands as you steward well what you are given. Jesus gives us the Parable of the Talents (money), where a man called his servants to manage his money for him while he is gone. Matthew 25:14-30 shows a parable (story) that how you handle what you are given is how you are allowed to grow because of the trust you demonstrate. The first two servants took the five talents and two talents and traded them and invested them and doubled what they were given. The third servant was given one talent and buried it, so when the owner came back, he gave him the buried talent back. The first two went to work applying what they were given. They used the purpose they had and went to work.

GOD HONORS YOU WHEN YOU GET TO WORK.

You are applying effort and heading in a direction that you are called to go in, even if you don't know all the pieces and might not fully understanding what you are doing, but you get going. Then there is that third servant. I'm only speculating here, but maybe he only got one and was insecure and didn't know what to do and how to apply effort. He thought it was best to just bury his talent, bury his calling, to sit on it and wait till he was clearly told how to apply what he was given. There are too many people that are just out here surviving, burying their talents because it doesn't fit within their current life structure. Maybe your purpose/calling doesn't fit into your current lifestyle, so you choose to make no space for it. It simply won't work until your obedience is being lived out. I have learned that the active ingredient in owning your purpose is simply obedience, even when it doesn't make sense in the moment. Your obedience will sometimes feel strange but necessary. It will sometimes hurt but be so valuable through the process. It will make sense someday, when you are looking back. There are so many things that I fought throughout my life when I was living a life that was purposeful to my will. God was slowly removing things that just didn't fit in the life where I was being called to go. You won't understand the people that are no longer in your daily circle. That doesn't mean that they don't hold importance to your life, but they are not going to ensure that you are headed in the direction that you are called to move. Looking back, it becomes easy to see the work and the paths that God has been developing in my life. The old thought that hindsight is 20/20 offers so much truth. You can see how God adjusted and influenced your life, the impact that your purpose offered to those around you, and the joy it gives you.

Passions and purpose go hand in hand with your life. The value you place on them is key.

IF YOUR PASSIONS OUTWEIGH YOUR PURPOSE, YOU ARE ALWAYS GOING TO BE CHASING THE NEXT THING.

You will never be content in what you have and how you live. Just being transparent here, but this is something I have to address and be aware of daily. I have to die (I know it's a strong concept), but you have to die to self-desires and seek God's will first to make a movement in God's direction for your life. In Luke 9:23 Jesus says, "And He was saying to them all, 'If anyone wishes to come after Me, he must deny himself, and take up his cross daily and follow Me.'" Jesus is giving us the simple directive to give up what we want first, a daily self-review to follow Him. God will give you the desires of your heart, but when you prove that He is your priority and when you demonstrate that you are seeking His will and you are owning your purpose each and every day. It's a lifestyle, not a one moment action. The choice is yours. We get to give all we've got and give up our will to live our purpose out, which is what we are here for.

REFLECTION SECTION

WHAT ARE YOU PASSIONATE ABOUT?

_____

_____

_____

_____

DO YOU FEEL THAT YOUR PURPOSE AND PASSIONS ARE IN THE RIGHT ORDER?

_____

_____

_____

_____

NOTES:

_____

_____

_____

_____

9

A NEW NORMAL

Get rid of the reminders and remnants of the old; let go and move on! Seems like such a bold statement and sounds so simple, but it is not. Let the new become the normal in your life. There are so many key thoughts and examples of letting the unique experiences you have become ordinary parts of everyday life. Experiences are to learn from. Both good and bad experiences help shape you along the way if you let them. Learn from positive experiences to know what to replicate in life; while negative experiences tell you what to avoid next time. In turn, you can help others recognize and share ideas and your experiences to help people avoid or go through what you can help them understand because of what you have experienced.

Making things normal is easy for some and really hard for others. Children often have no problem with this. Think

131

of Christmas morning. A few years ago, our kids came running in to wake us up, telling us it was Christmas time! Our oldest son was 10 or 11, and they must have peeked into the living room and seen all the presents around the tree, so we had to get up. We had to get the matching Christmas pajamas picture ready and have some breakfast while they tore apart their stockings to see what they had gotten. We tried hard to get them to take turns opening up all the presents, organized chaos was the goal. It's when they got done that the oldest boys said something funny. "Can we go to the store and get this other video game that we wanted?" Had the excitement worn off this quickly? Obviously, we didn't go toy shopping on Christmas, but within a very short time, all their new toys had become normal. They really acted for the most part like all the new toys were just standard now, like they have had them for a while and they were ready for something else. They started asking for new toys when they finished opening the ones they got hours ago. I'm actually a bit jealous that they could implement all this novelty in their lives so quickly. I am not the same way. I have some fishing tackle that I bought last year because I had to have it for the season but could never bring myself to use it. Some things I didn't even open until the next season; it was like it would lose its excitement if I used it. It's sad. I mean, if I did use it and it caught me more fish, I could buy another one. You would think it should be simple, but I have done it with clothing, food, toys, or whatever. I would just let it expire or outgrow it because there was a chance, I might ruin it. It is so weird that some of us would rather hoard things than enjoy them. I don't know what caused me to hold on to new things rather than use them. It could be because I watched everyone struggle with acquiring new items. I would work hard and buy what I wanted, but I desired to have it rather than use it.

God gives us gifts and sometimes we hold onto them and don't use them. The gifts from God are for us to use, and like anything, you can lose what you don't use and experience. Romans 11:29-31 says, "For the gifts and the calling of God are irrevocable. For just as you once were disobedient to God, but now have been shown mercy because of their disobedience, so these also now have been disobedient, that because of the mercy shown to you, they also may now be shown mercy." God is not going to change His mind on your assignment. It says it is irrevocable. God will not take back what He has called you to do. So many times, I have run from what I should have been doing, yet God knew what it was going to take for me to answer my calling. It was going to take the right timing, the right people, and the right environment to cultivate and grow what God intended for me the whole time. All the interactions with the right people and the timing of the exposure proved that God was lining things up the entire time. I have found that childlike acceptance of all the new in my life.

In Matthew 6:14-15 it says, "For if you forgive others for their transgressions, your heavenly Father will also forgive you. But if you do not forgive others, then your Father will not forgive your transgressions." Forgiveness is so crucial to living life in the new normal. We have to let go and forgive others. It clearly shows us here that we must forgive others before God will forgive us.

IF WE WANT TO LIVE A PURPOSEFUL LIFE, THEN WE MUST FORGIVE AND LET GO SO GOD CAN MOVE US FORWARD.

Here in Mark 11:24-25, this is repeated. The gospels are an account of all the significant things that Jesus says and are critical for us to understand. "Whenever you stand praying, forgive if you have anything against anyone so that your Father who is in heaven will also forgive you your transgressions. [But if you do not forgive, neither will your Father who is in heaven forgive your transgressions."] You cannot own your purpose if you are holding yourself back with unforgiveness. One more example of this in Ephesians 4:31-32 where Paul says, "Let all bitterness and wrath and anger and clamor and slander be put away from you, along with all malice. Be kind to one another, tender-hearted, and forgive each other, just as God in Christ has forgiven you."

I remember this moment like it was yesterday. I was a young teenager, and we all went to visit some family members. It was a trip where we always spent a night at one house and then took a short drive to the other house and stayed a night or two there. Well, just like any trip we poured out of the truck and ran into the house, probably because I had to run to the bathroom because it had been 30 minutes since the last stop. I'm probably the worst person to travel with and often have to stop once an hour unless I don't drink anything. When I was kid, it was no different. If I've got to go, I've got to hurry. Looking back at this, it was regrettable that I had to overhear what I did. But that being said, I did have to experience it. I overheard my dad talking to this relative that we came to visit and she made it very clear that us greasy-headed kids would not be sleeping on her pillows. What did I hear? I could not believe it, and I went out the front door and to the truck. I can still remember how I felt so frustrated and extremely mad. I was hurt and embarrassed, and no way would I be going back into that house. My dad came outside and told me to get inside, it was getting late. I told him what I had heard, and that no way would I ever step foot back inside that house. I was wounded and so hurt. Of course, my dad insisted, but I can distinctly remember this was the first time I told him definitively no way, that he could beat me if he needed to, but no way was I going back in, ever. I'm sad to say I didn't let this go, and I never did step back into

OWN YOUR PURPOSE

that house. This hatred and unforgiveness followed me for a long time. Years later, my parents asked if I could come down for a weekend and help them move from their home. I came to help my dad and mom because they asked me to and of course I showed up. I rode BMX daily, so of course, I had my bike with me, and everyone decided to take a break for a little bit. This family member showed up and decided to verbally attack me again, saying she could not believe that I would be "playing" on my bike when I should be helping. Why me? What did I ever do to this woman that would cause so much unkindness, seemingly aimed at me? I learned that she treated many other people the same way, but that did not excuse any of it. So, like any young adult, I was being respectful until I opened my mouth. I let her know that I did not come to help her, nor would I have shown up if it was to help her. I know this all sounds bad, but there is a point. I told her that I came to help my parents, not her. I chose to spend my time off helping my parents and that was the end of it. I was going to ride my bike while everyone was sitting around enjoying some downtime. She stomped to her car to drive to my parents' other home to tell them how awful I was and had just treated her. I didn't care. I grabbed my younger sister and went to have lunch. During lunch the other family member strolled into the store, gave me a high-five, and said a few choice words, but to summarize she said she would have done the same thing. It was a proud moment for all the wrong reasons. A family event a few years later brought us in the same room together again. I was compassionate and kind but

136

guarded. I didn't want to keep it all going, but I still did not understand why I was treated the way I was for so many years. It was several years again in 2018 when I gave my heart to Jesus that I learned these key scripture passages. For God to forgive me, I had to forgive. It doesn't mean that this family member changed, but I did. God changed something in my heart that makes all the difference. He allowed me to move past the unforgiveness and towards what He called me to. There is no longer an ill feeling towards her; God has shown me compassion for her. I don't know what has caused her frustrations or caused her to treat me the way she did, but it's all good now. It never needs to be opened but demonstrates that you cannot move on if you hold on to unforgiveness. The situations surrounding it will keep coming up until it has been dealt with. Hebrews 8:12 shows us that all is new. "For I will be merciful to their iniquities, And I will remember their sins no more." God wants the best for us; our purpose is the best version of life God has for us, and unforgiveness is just one thing that we have to deal with. We need this freedom so it doesn't limit our relationship with God and the freedom to walk into and own your purpose.

Every day, we hear and see so much information. We are bombarded with sounds and images everywhere. The average person watches at least five hours of TV a day. This includes video games, just in case you don't think they count. With the average person hearing over 100,000 words a day (the equivalent of a 300-page book consumed daily), that is a lot of information to filter, process, or ignore. If you add in images and other sounds, it is over 30 gigabytes of information. This is just the average. If you engage in a public setting, attend school or simply being are social, you could be exceeding the average. I am constantly being told that I have selective hearing. Maybe this is not bad if I only caught all the important stuff. Just with words you hear, you are forced to process about 104 words a minute if awake 16 hours a day. This is so much info. What do you retain, use, or learn from that you take into your life and make normal? It seems funny to me to say it this way, but in all reality you are almost always in learning mode. What you hear you can choose to make normal by actively applying it to your life. The brain retains information like your muscles retain strength; you lose it if you don't use it. For the life of me, I cannot remember how to do calculus even though I took the class twice. I never used it so it has fallen somewhere in the back of my brain and is currently unimportant. However, I think that if I got a quick overview, I could remember it again. Anti-derivatives don't mean anything currently, but I might dig into a refresher if I get bored. That is a big maybe.

When you are in church and receive from the Holy Spirit, how do you ensure that all that is new stays with you Monday-Saturday, using the latest that you received on Sunday? The message may speak to you, and you spend the week applying what you have learned. Maybe the worship wrecked you and showed you some new accountability measures you feel convicted to apply. All too often we fall back to the way we were on our journey back through the parking lot to our vehicles. If you don't let these new revelations become normal in your life, you will always be held back from receiving freedom in this new you were given.

Throughout the Bible there are so many examples of this thought, "making your new normal." Jesus cures a man of dropsy, even though it was on the Sabbath and people weren't allowed to do such acts. Dropsy is an old term used to describe body swelling. It is often associated with heart failure and other heart conditions. In Luke 14:1-4 it tells the story. "One Sabbath, when Jesus went to eat in the house of a prominent Pharisee, he was being carefully watched. There in front of him was a man suffering from abnormal body swelling. Jesus asked the Pharisees and experts in the law, 'Is it lawful to heal on the Sabbath or not?' But they remained silent. So, taking hold of the man, he healed and sent him on his way." This man was healed at a time that was thought not to be okay because it was on the Sabbath. This man's whole life was changed in a moment. Jesus just came across his path saw the situation and changed his life. The man could have just denied what happened and stayed put out of fear that nothing changed, and everything stayed the same. That isn't what happened. Instead, he accepted his healing. He took off into the new and received what Jesus gave him in his life.

I have had severe knee pain for years, dating back to

injuries in 2002 and 2003. In 2003, I tore my ACL from falling six feet down on a 7' spine mini ramp, not taking seriously the trick I was performing. This was a trick I had done several times on a BMX bike. I fell from the top to the bottom of the ramp and my knee folded backwards, tearing my ACL partially. A couple of days later, I was feeling a little less pain, so I got back on the bike and jumped down a handrail that was on the outside of a set of ramps. I landed it on the first try but slid off the rail, and it felt sloppy to me, so I tried again. This time, I barely hit the rail because I jumped out too far and slipped off my right pedal, slamming my foot to the ground. At this point, I tore my ACL completely. It was so painful. I was at a training camp on the East Coast so I was headed back to my cabin. It began to rain, so my bike slipped out from underneath me and I fell down a slippery concrete hill right unto my tailbone breaking it as well. It was quite the evening. I ended up leaving camp a couple of weeks early and going back to my job, awaiting surgery on my knee. I had the surgery in October 2003 and was told that it would be at least a year before I was back on the bike. I got cleared to ride again, and I was around riding in February of 2004. The doctor was surprised that it was 100% good to go but he said to go for it. By summer I was riding six days a week again, but I started to develop a lot of pain in my right knee, the one I had surgery on.

Over the next few years, it only got worse and was always bothering me. I have seen doctors and specialists and have found that I have developed arthritis in my knee and need a knee replacement to correct the problem. Every flight I have taken over the years, my knee bothered me for the whole day afterwards. It just became something I accepted as part of my "new normal." God doesn't expect our pain and frustration to be part of our normal. In June of 2022, 19 years later, I am still dealing with lots of knee pain and was getting ready for a trip to Miami. This time, with a different mindset and with authority that is given to us through Jesus, I told God that I knew the knee pain was gone and I wasn't going to have to deal with it anymore at all. I left for our trip and landed in Miami. The next day, I realized what had happened. The knee pain was completely gone. I could not wait to share the news with everyone that knew that I have been dealing with this pain for so long. For the first time in 19 years, I have had no knee pain. It has been almost a year and half later now, and I still have no pain.

IT'S AMAZING WHAT HAPPENS WHEN YOU REACH OUT IN FAITH TO GOD, AND HE RELEASES WHAT HE HAS FOR YOU.

Something that I have dealt with for so long, and it was gone in an instant. Looking at this whole timeline, the healing was there the entire time; I just didn't have the faith to make the new normal. I accepted the current situation and didn't look at the blessing that was there for the taking. What have you received from God that is just waiting for you to acknowledge you have? Embrace the new and release what God has for you to live within your life. Owning your purpose will require you to constantly embrace what is new and what is unfolding in front of you. It will take decisions to step into the unknown and walk in faith all the time.

In Luke 17:11-19, Jesus cleansed ten lepers. If you aren't familiar with leprosy, the disease is a bacterial infection. The number of lesions and sores that lepers have to deal with were intense, painful and left scars all over their bodies. It almost resembles spots like a leopard has. Lepers had to follow strict guidelines about contact with and their proximity to others. Walking around, they had to yell "unclean, unclean" everywhere they went. They would have to wear torn clothing and cover part of their faces as they would embarrass themselves, declaring what they were known as. Their issue became their identity. They were lepers, people with issues that needed to be separated from all. Back in the biblical times, cities often had walls and gates and lepers where usually not even allowed in the cities or the camps. They were isolated from everyone.

The text referenced in Luke 17 states this: "Now, on his way to Jerusalem, Jesus traveled along the border between

Samaria and Galilee. As he was going into a village, ten men who had leprosy met him. They stood at a distance and called out in a loud voice, 'Jesus, Master, have pity on us!' When he saw them, he said, 'Go, show yourselves to the priests.' And as they went, they were cleansed. One of them, when he saw he was healed, came back, praising God in a loud voice. He threw himself at Jesus' feet and thanked him—and he was a Samaritan. Jesus asked, 'Were not all ten cleansed? Where are the other nine? Has no one returned to give praise to God except this foreigner?' Then he said to him, 'Rise and go; your faith has made you well.'" I love this. The only person to return was the Samaritan, a non-Jewish person. When they yelled to Jesus, they only asked for pity. Then Jesus told them to go see the priests. As they went to the priests out of obedience, they began to change, to be cleansed. They were given something new through their obedience and they were cleansed, made new.

Only one of them came back to praise Jesus for the gift of health and freedom to not be alone anymore. Isolation, whether because you have to or because you choose to be alone, is hard. It changes you; it keeps you from fulfilling what you are here for.

NO ONE IS ON EARTH TO LIVE ALONE, TO BE SEPARATED FROM COMMUNITY.

Everyone belongs in a group that will encourage you, help you develop and keep you accountable. When you are making the new normal, you are allowing God to know you are progressing and growing and want more. If you do not accept or use God's gifts, you are going to lose them. If you don't let God change or transform you, He will transfer the responsibility to the next available person. We already talked about this, but Saul could not make the cut and gave into his flesh over and over again, and God then passed the blessing unto David.

Start making the new normal. When it's time for church, we need to be prepared to receive and apply what we learn so we are ready for the next week. Too many times we come to church and beg for just enough to get over the last week and then repeat again the upcoming week. We need to stop pulling into church like it's a gas station and we had to push the car to the pump to add some gas into it to leave the station. We're on empty so much that the vehicle barely wants to start because it is so dry and barren. The tires are all on low air pressure, and you just took the jumper cables off because the battery wasn't charged. Now imagine what it's like if we treat it differently. We check our tires weekly to ensure that the pressure is good. We update the battery when it is starting to not hold the charge like it used to. We get gas routinely, so we don't go under a certain amount. We can always get to church because all week we have been doing the daily maintenance to live in the new we have received. We read the Bible, pray, reach out to others when we struggle; we call to Jesus when we need His pity. Jesus will give me all I need when I seek Him and always reach out to Him. When things are good, reach out with thanks. When things are tough, reach out to God. When we reach out to God, when we are living for Him, God will always show up and show out. We must live each day representing our God and seeking Him daily with all He has given us.

One of the biggest challenges of letting the new normal in your life is how you feel about yourself. Self-hatred is so fundamental to this problem because we have such a hard time feeling like we deserve good things. We claim that we don't deserve God's love, we are nobody, and we made too many mistakes to be used by God, to have a purpose that we are called to fulfill and live out. I spent many years in this mindset. My biological father walked out on our lives when we were little. I remember the feeling of "What did I do to deserve him leaving?" I could see him, and yet he didn't want me. How could a God that I can't even see love me so much when my dad couldn't? We are blinded by how we see ourselves. We shy away from our callings because we let our insecurities hold us back from allowing God to make His gifts come to life. If we choose to use them and own our purpose with God's help, it reveals that we are worth it. It helps us find peace in seeking a way to forgive ourselves and to let self-hatred go. Proverbs 19:8 shows us how to love ourselves. "To acquire wisdom is to love yourself; people who cherish understanding will prosper." Making the new normal is precisely this. Applying learned wisdom is loving yourself. You cannot fully accept the new if you don't let your insecurities go and love yourself as God loves you.

REFLECTION SECTION

WHAT HAVE YOU LEARNED THAT YOU ARE NOT APPLYING IN YOUR LIFE?

_____

_____

_____

_____

WHAT NEEDS TO CHANGE?

_____

_____

_____

WHAT ARE YOU HOLDING ONTO THAT YOU NEED TO FORGIVE YOURSELF FOR?

_____

_____

_____

_____

147

WHO CAN YOU REACH OUT TO WHEN YOU FEEL ALONE?

_____

_____

_____

WORK THROUGH SOME OF THESE QUESTIONS TO HELP ENSURE YOUR NEW BECOMES NORMAL IN YOUR LIFE.

_____

_____

_____

NOTES:

_____

_____

_____

_____

_____

_____

_____

10

DISRUPT THE ROOM

There are several disruptive people throughout the Bible, and their purpose called them into action, to not sit idle and let the world pass them by but to change the world around them.

YOUR PURPOSE IS CALLING YOU TO DISRUPT THE ROOM, CALLING YOU INTO ACTION TO ADD VALUE TO YOUR SURROUNDINGS AND NOT TO SIT IN THE CORNER, LETTING LIFE HAPPEN.

In Mark 16:15-16 it says, "And He said to them, 'Go into all the world and preach the gospel to all creation. He who has believed and has been baptized shall be saved, but he who has disbelieved shall be condemned.'" If this isn't a call to be disruptive, I don't know what is. We are called to go out and preach the gospel. I want to share the story of Jesus to help people see that their current trajectory will only get them so far without Him.

Hebrews 6: 17-18 says, "In the same way God, desiring even more to show to the heirs of the promise the unchangeableness of His purpose, interposed with an oath, so that by two unchangeable things in which it is impossible for God to lie, we who have taken refuge would have strong encouragement to take hold of the hope set before us." If God tells you that He needs you to do something or that you are made for something, then it is so. Your purpose is designed for you and if you are called to something, then own your purpose and by all means disrupt the room.

Moses is indeed miraculous. It is the story of a Hebrew boy who lived amongst the Egyptians and should have never been allowed to live only to be called to disrupt the world around him. His calling was to change the lives of the Hebrews that he was born from and raised with the knowledge of the Egyptians and the Hebrew enslaved people. In Exodus 1: 15-22, the Egyptian Pharoah called on the Hebrew midwives to kill all the male babies when they were born. Suppose it was a girl, then let her live. They refused to do this, so the Hebrews multiplied and grew in numbers. The Pharoah questioned the midwives but with quick thinking they told the Pharoah that the Hebrew women went into labor and had their babies quickly on their own. God blessed the midwives for protecting the boy children, which allowed Moses to be born safety. In Exodus 2, they talk about Moses being born and hiding him for three months until they could no longer hide him. They placed him in a wicker basket and covered it with tar and pitch to waterproof it. I'm sure that they had no idea at the time that this basket was going to be such a critical vessel, carrying the one that would eventually lead the Hebrews to freedom from the Egyptians. The tar and pitch was probably the same material used on Noah's Ark in Genesis. What a miracle it was for a three-month-old baby to be placed in a basket, floated off to be found by the Pharaoh's daughter, and then given back to his mother to be raised and weaned till he was ready to move to the palace as the son of the Pharoah's daughter.

As Moses grew up, he saw the unjust behavior that the Hebrews were under. One day when he was 40 years old, he witnessed an Egyptian attack a Hebrew enslaved person. Something rose up in him and he attacked and killed the Egyptian and disposed of the body. Word got out quickly, and when Pharoah heard what had happened, he tried to have Moses killed. At this point, Moses disappeared into the wilderness, running away from all he knew and was familiar with. Moses spent the next 40 years in the wilderness, preparing himself for the subsequent phases in his life. God sometimes will send you to the wilderness to prepare for what's next. You hear people saying, "I'm in a tough season." Or maybe everything is great, and they are doing well. Moses was in a tough season. He was a murderer; he fled everything he knew in fear of the unknown. He didn't know the people, how to fend for himself, etc. Your wilderness can be a place of zero comfort, facing the unknown. It can feel lonely, and if you let it control you, it can distort the purpose you are there for. Every season, good or bad, has a purpose you can learn from and let it develop you if you allow it.

In Exodus 3:10-13 says, "'Therefore, come now, and I will send you to Pharaoh, so that you may bring My people, the sons of Israel, out of Egypt.' But Moses said to God, 'Who am I, that I should go to Pharaoh, and that I should bring the sons of Israel out of Egypt?' And He said, 'Certainly I will be with you, and this shall be the sign to you that it is I who have sent you: when you have brought the people out of Egypt, you shall worship God at this mountain.'"

Moses was insecure and unsure of himself and tried to rationalize with God because he thought God must have it wrong. God cannot be wrong. It's impossible. Moses complained to God that he was unqualified, not equipped, not ready for what was next. You are not going to be comfortable with what you are called into. If you can do it on your own, you are calling yourself and it's not big enough for the version God has for you. At this point, Moses got his directive to be disruptive and set God's people free from their bondage under Pharoah. When Moses went back to Egypt, it was under different leadership than when he left. The conditions that he ran from were not any better; yet even though the leaders were different, the calling stayed the same: lead the rescue of My people from Egypt. Go in there and disrupt all that the Hebrew slaves know.

God promises action and talks to Moses. In Exodus 6:1, "Then the Lord said to Moses, 'Now you shall see what I will do to Pharaoh; for under compulsion he will let them go, and under compulsion, he will drive them out of his land.'" Moses meets with the Pharaoh and tells him what God has said, and then crazy stuff started to happen. One by one, the Egyptians are faced with plagues that ravaged their territory. God begins the plagues, first by turning water to blood. Followed by plagues of frogs, lice, flies. Next all the livestock were to die, and people were tormented by boils, hail, and locusts. Up until this point, Pharoah repeatedly refused to let the Hebrew enslaved people go, but the locusts crossed a line. It was then that God began to harden Pharaoh's heart. God wanted to make sure that there was no question that He was the reason for this and that He alone would be the reason that the Pharoah would let the people go. The plagues continued with total darkness, and finally, the killing of the firstborn. This was a reflection of Pharaoh's command 80 years earlier when Moses was born and escaped into the Nile that all the boys born to the Hebrew slaves should not be allowed to live so the population could be controlled.

Talk about disruptive to the life of Pharoah and the Egyptians! The plagues all had to happen because God was fulfilling a promise He made to Abraham in Genesis. In Genesis 15:13-14 it says, "God said to Abram, 'Know for certain that your descendants will be strangers in a land that is not theirs, where they will be enslaved and oppressed for four hundred years. But I will also judge the nation whom they will serve, and afterward, they will come out with many possessions.'"

We are called into action and to be disruptive in our lives. If we are not, then our silence is the greatest gift to the devil. He would like nothing more than for us to stay silent, not seek out our purpose, and not impact the world around us as we are called to do. Being disruptive while being led by Jesus will make mountains move, the blind see, and water turn into wine. In John 2:3-6, 8-10 we see Mary, Jesus' mother, and Jesus disrupting the room when only a few servants even notice. "When the wine ran out, the mother of Jesus said to Him, 'They have no wine.' And Jesus said to her, 'Woman, what does that have to do with us? My hour has not yet come.' His mother said to the servants, 'Whatever He says to you, do it.' Now, there were six stone waterpots set there for the Jewish custom of purification, containing twenty or thirty gallons each. 'Fill the waterpots with water.' So, they filled them up to the brim. And He said to them, 'Draw some out now and take it to the headwaiter.' So, they took it to him. When the headwaiter tasted the water which had become wine and did not know where it came from (but the servants who had drawn the water knew), the headwaiter called the bridegroom and said to him, 'Every man serves the good wine first, and when the people have drunk freely, then he serves the poorer wine; but you have kept the good wine until now.'" Anything Jesus touches will be better than what came before it. When God is leading you, you can only imagine the success of your output. You already have all you need. Jesus can take what you have that seems unimportant to you and turn it into the best version of what people need.

Living disruptively is going to have some obvious tells, key indicators that you are in your purpose and making an impact.

SOME PEOPLE ARE DRAWN TO YOU OR REPELLED BY YOU; THIS IS HOW YOU KNOW YOU ARE LIVING DISRUPTIVELY.

God causes this favor in your life, and the people that interact with you in your purpose will choose to benefit or run from what you have to share. God will give you the tools needed for this to happen. Disruptive behavior causes the environment to change when you enter a room; the Holy Spirit will cause favor on you to change your environment when you trust Him to do so.

This is an easy, practical example of being disruptive. When it has rained, you decide to go for a walk outside. You come up to a puddle, and you are contemplating whether you are going to jump into it, step on it lightly to not splash, or go around it.   If you jump in the puddle, the disruption can be epic. You could splash yourself and anything in your proximity. You could make people happy or frustrated depending on when and where this disruptive event occurs. Instead of jumping into the puddle you might step into it. It is still disrupted but very subtle movement except for the ripples from the impact of your shoe. No matter how carefully you step, it will still cause a ripple effect that disrupts the surface of the water. You can stroll around the puddle, but it is still disruptive. If you go around a puddle on a busy sidewalk, you may cause someone else to get their feet wet. You could step somewhere that isn't stable and you may trip, or maybe it forces you to fall and you go all in on that puddle. Now, your plans are all disrupted and have completely changed from what you set out for this particular day. Obviously, none of this could have happened or every bit of it could. Being disruptive will impact everything around you and does not always require a vast movement or action to be noticed. Do you find yourself avoiding puddles or jumping in to have the most significant impact possible? You change by the day, but your impact matters. Your influence matters. When you own your purpose, it will be disruptive and make a mark where it is supposed to.

Being disruptive can also look like this. I was pulling into the outside right lane of a double-lane fast food drive through, and a guy started to obsessively honk his horn because he thought I was going to cut him off and pull into the left lane ahead of him. Doing the bravest thing I could, I complained that this guy was acting way out of line, because he had no idea what I was actually going to do. So, I would like to think now it was the Holy Spirit speaking to me, but it could have easily been me thinking "I'm going to make this guy feel like a real jerk and I will pay for his meal from the other lane." So, I waved sarcastically to the guy and proceeded to pull up to the pay window and paid for our meal and then asked if I could pay for his. The look on the guy's face was shocked, that after how he treated me, I would pay for his meal. He was waving out his window and I could faintly hear him yelling "thank you" as I drove away. As I drove away smiling, a feeling of good started to take over. Not like "I got you," like "Wow, that was the right thing to do." I completely disrupted this guy's day. I had no idea what he was going through. Maybe he was just in an argument or a fight, whatever could have put him on edge. My frustration turned into a blessing for someone else, then it happened. God disrupted my day through my children. One of my sons said, "Dad, that guy was rude and you bought his meal? Why would you be nice to someone who wasn't nice to you?" This boy taught his dad a lesson. School was in session. I mean, I had no idea he was even paying attention while buried into whatever game he was playing on his phone. There was so much disruption going on that looking back, God used my son teach me that day. Your children are always watching and are students of your actions and behaviors. Disruption is not a form of manipulation. When you are living disruptively, you're changing the flow of whatever current situation you walk into. It's based on love and encouragement, not on selfish gain.

Another example from the Bible is the men who tore the roof open to lower their friend down in front of Jesus. They knew if they could disrupt the service to get their friend to Jesus, he would be healed. It's funny, because here they had the faith for their friend; it doesn't say that he asked them to get him to Jesus. They knew what their friend needed, that he needed an encounter with the One Who can change any situation. Here in Luke 5: 17-25 it says, "One day He was teaching; and there were some Pharisees and teachers of the law sitting there, who had come from every village of Galilee and Judea and from Jerusalem; and the power of the Lord was present for Him to perform healing. And some men were carrying on a bed a man who was paralyzed, and they were trying to bring him in and to set him down in front of Him. But not finding any way to bring him in because of the crowd, they went up on the roof and let him down through the tiles with his stretcher into the middle of the crowd, in front of Jesus. Seeing their faith, He said, 'Friend, your sins are forgiven.' The scribes and the Pharisees began to reason, saying, 'Who is this man who speaks blasphemies? Who can forgive sins but God alone?' But Jesus, aware of their reasonings, answered and said to them, 'Why are you reasoning in your hearts? Which is easier, to say, "Your sins have been forgiven you," or to say, "Get up and walk"? But so that you may know that the Son of Man has authority on earth to forgive sins,'—He said to the paralytic— 'I say to you, get up, and pick up your stretcher and go home.' Immediately he got up before them, and picked up what he had been lying on, and went home glorifying God." Here again Jesus was being disruptive and forgiving this man's sins, and then says, "Rise up you are healed." Religious mindset will always say that is not how it should have been done. That's not the way it's always done. Being disruptive sometimes makes people say it shouldn't work that way, or "That's not how I was taught." Anytime I can learn a new way to do something I can already do, it fascinates me. Especially if it saves me time.

In Matthew 21:12-14, Jesus disrupts a whole lot of religious corruption. "And Jesus entered the temple and drove out all those who were buying and selling in the temple, and overturned the tables of the money changers and the seats of those who were selling doves. And He said to them, 'It is written, "My house shall be called a house of prayer;" but you are making it a robbers' den.' And the blind and the lame came to Him in the temple, and He healed them." He calls out the evil, flips over the tables spilling their money and supplies everywhere, and then starts healing people all over the place. I love to imagine this scene live; what a scene it must have been. Are you willing to be disruptive like this in your life? To be like Jesus called us to be, disruptive with Him first through salvation and then accepting Holy Spirit living in us? The most disruptive act we can experience in our personal life is to accept Jesus through salvation and then accept the call from Jesus, by owning your purpose.

WHEN YOU LET JESUS WORK IN YOUR LIFE, EXPECT A DISRUPTION, EXPECT THINGS TO CHANGE AND NOT STAY TO THE SAME.

Let the Holy Spirit dwell and live in and through you. We are called to stand apart from this world, to be different, to be disruptive. When you are in your purpose, you will not be comfortable in the same circles you used to be. You will be drawn to people who will support you, encourage you, and help you get to where you are supposed to go. Disrupters approach life with a shovel, not a rake. A rake adjusts the surface, the part that everyone can see. A shovel, on the other hand, will dig past the surface and not only stirs things up but will expose things that need to change, areas in your life that you need for your purpose that maybe you could not see before. Prayers like this are dangerous and vulnerable but will impact you significantly. God, pick me apart with a shovel. Expose what You want me to develop and change, but show me that I have what I need for You to move forward within my purpose.

Miracles are answers to prayer, but blessings are an unexpected disruption. Blessings should never be the motive behind the purpose. You will never achieve owning your purpose if you are only doing this to get that. Both miracles and blessings are beautiful and can change your life so much. Your purpose will lead you through seasons that are disruptive and harsh at times. When we look at these seasons, we have a choice. We can let them control us, or we can seek what these challenging times are all about.

May 7-28, 2023, marked a 21-day fast a group started online, with over 1 million people joining in prayer and fasting for the people of Israel. Talk about disruptive. They had no idea at the beginning it was going to get this much traction, but you cannot get much more disruptive than over a million people fasting and praying for the nation of Israel.

I briefly mentioned salvation in Jesus Christ and surrendering your life totally to Him, letting God direct you in your purpose, guiding your steps, lifting you up when needed, and nudging you forward when you are struggling. The relationship you have with Jesus is a choice, and how you work towards getting to know Him intimately is going to make all the difference. You can ask God into your life by acknowledging your sins, asking forgiveness, and inviting God to live in you.

GOD WANTS YOU AS YOU ARE, BUT THE MORE YOU GET TO KNOW HIM, THE MORE YOU WILL SEE THAT HE DOESN'T WANT TO LEAVE YOU THE WAY YOU ARE.

There is so much freedom in letting God lead your life. You will get it wrong daily, but nobody is perfect. Nobody gets it all right all the time. The next step in your relationship with God is to live life being led by the Holy Spirit.

When the disciples were waiting in the upper room, everything changed. In Acts 2:2-4 it states:

"And suddenly there came from heaven a noise like a violent rushing wind, and it filled the whole house where they were sitting. And there appeared to them tongues as of fire distributing themselves, and they rested on each one of them. And they were all filled with the Holy Spirit and began to speak with other tongues, as the Spirit was giving them utterance." You owning your purpose with God, Jesus, and the Holy Spirit taking the lead, directing your paths, will give you the best fulfilled life. It won't always be easy, and will not be without challenging seasons.

Take a leap of faith and live a disruptive life. Be bold and challenge those around you. Share your faith every chance you get. Give God your all, and you will be blown away by what your life becomes. God will give you all you need to fulfill your purpose.

Trust God in what He is calling you to do, even if you don't feel qualified, well-spoken, whatever. You might think that it makes no sense that God is looking to you to fulfill what God is calling you to do. Could you take the following steps towards it? God is calling you to your purpose and looking for your obedience. A lot of times, failure comes by walking in disobedience.

The purpose of this book has been to help you find the challenges of living a purpose-filled life, to eliminate the challenges and excuses you keep running to when it gets tricky. When it all seems unlikely that anything is coming of what we are trying to achieve, God will be there waiting for you to call on Him, so with His help, all will begin to make sense. We need to remember that God knows our beginning and our end. In Revelations 1:8, God says, "'I am the Alpha and the Omega,' says the Lord God, 'who is and who was and who is to come, the Almighty.'" God knows what we are going to do, where we are going to trust Him, and where we are going to fall short. Owning your purpose is your choice. God gives us the choice and the means to fulfill His purpose for us. Make decisions on purpose and go out there and own your purpose.

REFLECTION SECTION

DO YOU FEEL THAT YOU WERE
CALLED TO DISRUPT SOMETHING
THAT YOU DIDN'T?

_____

_____

_____

_____

WHAT ROOMS HAVE YOU WALKED
INTO THAT YOU JUST SAT IN THE
CORNER AND BLENDED IN?

_____

_____

_____

_____

NOTES:

_____

_____

_____

_____

A CHAPTER IN YOUR FUTURE— WHAT NOW?

I have written this book in hopes that it will speak to you, give you some ideas of what is holding you back, or simply reassure you that you are not the only one struggling with life in general, trying to living out your purpose as you are called to do. I have poured into these pages my thoughts, and I am hopeful you have been inspired to press into what God has for you. It's an amazing feeling, to know that even though I'm at the end of this journey developing a book through the inspiration God has shared with me, that the journey has only just begun.

Living a life on purpose, intently making decisions that are deliberately focused on heading in the direction that you feel God is taking you, is so important. Seek God for understanding.

GOD KNOWS WHAT HE DID BY CALLING YOU INTO ACTION FOR A TIME AND SEASON THAT IS RIGHT NOW.

You are the exact person needed for the calling. God knows you received it when you are trusting in Him to get you there. Saul lost his anointing due to his disobedience in failing to fulfill his purpose; David was anointed and eventually came to the challenge of Goliath which Saul ignored for 40 days. David fulfilled a role that was not his fight; it was Saul's the whole time. Don't give your calling away because you will not head in the direction you feel called to go. God will always accomplish what needs to be done, and sometimes God goes to His second choice because we don't step up to what we are being called to do. If you are struggling to do something that feels so right for God and you have to pray your way through it daily, then you are most likely on the right path. The devil will mess with you in so many ways when you are focused on going the way God wants. If you aren't focused on what God wants for your life, you are no threat in that moment. This leads us to realizing that easy street is real, because if it is too easy, God has so much more for you.

Our insecurities can be so loud at times. We can lose focus and be distracted in our lives if we are constantly doubting and second guessing the steps we are taking. Insecurities will rob you if you let them be the loudest voices you are listening to. I have spent so much of my life listening to those loud voices for way too long, making choices and decisions based on fear and lack of trust in God and my abilities. When you feel insecure: rise up, kneel down, reach out to God and seek His love and guidance. God gives you authority to silence the insecurities and the hold backs in your life. God wants us to be free of these strongholds and trust Him that we are being guided forward away from our insecurities. You will always face opportunities to confront insecurities. If you are struggling, reach out for guidance and prayer to get through whatever situation you are dealing with.

Are you seeking out friends and mentors who will support you and help develop you to strengthen your roots? Just like a palm tree is strengthened by the storms they are faced with growing into the stretch that the storms cause, we can learn from the storms that come into our lives. Palm trees in groups are much stronger because the roots are developed together and they tend to support each other. Get a group of friends that will strengthen you when you are weak and need someone to encourage you when you need the pick me up.

We are all called to lead. What or who are you leading? Is it at school, work, your church, your peers? We are all leaders in something. Who is leading you? Get a mentor or a counselor who will speak into your life all the time.

Challenge yourself to have a healthy work/rest life balance. Work and rest are mentioned all over the Bible. The first conversation we see in the Bible is Adam being given a purpose, to name the animals. God called us to get going and get to work. Your purpose is going to require you to do exactly that. God isn't just going to hand you whatever you want and poof! You are doing what you can handle and you are called to do. God knows what you can handle and that you are called to get focused on Him and get going. Your obedience in taking steps in a direction you believe you are called to go in does something special. It activates God to work on your behalf. Have you ever gone bowling and had them put up the bumpers on the lane? If you throw the bowling ball in the direction of the pins and get off course, rolling towards the gutters, the bumpers will prevent you from falling in by redirecting your ball back in the direction of the pins. I believe God is those bumpers in our life. You get going in the direction you believe you are supposed to go. You have an idea of the destination and you begin going that way. You start going off track and God will nudge you back towards the finish line. When you seek Him and ask for guidance from Him, He won't let you fall off course. You will get close; you might ride those bumpers only to get put back on track over and over again.

God's grace is sufficient for you to see your purpose come into action, no matter how messed up you think you are.

Disrupt the rooms you enter. You are not called to be a bench warmer, sitting in the corner and avoiding any chance to make an impact everywhere you go. God has called us disrupt the wrongdoing, to change the environments that we enter. Do people notice that you are different at school, work, when you shop in a store, driving your car? Do you go places and act like everyone else just to fit in, or are you different, so they wonder what you have? Are you screaming and acting out of character, borderline offensive, at sporting events right after you were acting so holy just a few hours before. Are you wearing masks everywhere you go to simply fit in? Or can people trust your character everywhere you are because you let the masks go, you smashed the personas that you believe people need from you, choosing to be who God has called you to be? Are you standing out and not trying to fit in, giving up self-centered behavior, and focusing on God's purpose for you?

Lastly, if this book has helped you in any way, share it. Share your story with someone.

GOD WANTS US TO SHARE WITH PEOPLE HOW HE IS CHANGING US.

God has done so much in my life and has changed how I think, act, and respond to all life brings my way. Seeking God through my choices and choosing to be obedient to His call on my life has been everything.

If you don't know God personally, and want to, it is so simple to get started. Simply say this prayer: "God, I'm broken and have been lost in my life. I've tried to do this life on my own. God, I'm asking for forgiveness of sins, acknowledging that I am a sinner. Jesus, come into my life, change me, make me aware of Your presence and don't leave me the same. In Jesus name I'm renewed in you. Amen!!"

If you have said this for the first time, or first time in a long time, it's time to celebrate you and your choice to follow Jesus. Get ahold of a Bible-believing church and get plugged in to Sunday service and any groups that you may be interested in. This will lead you to people that you can lean on and grow from. Grab a Bible and get reading. It is the one book guaranteed to read you back and you cannot help but be changed if you choose to apply it to your life.

THE NEXT CHAPTER IS UP TO YOU BE OBEDIENT AND OWN YOUR PURPOSE!

BIBLE REFERENCES

CHAPTER 1- ON PURPOSE

Luke 12:7

> *"Indeed, the very hairs of your head are all numbered. Do not fear; you are more valuable than many sparrows."*

Matthew 14:22-25

> *"Immediately He made the disciples get into the boat and go ahead of Him to the other side, while He sent the crowds away. After He had sent the crowds away, He went up on the mountain by Himself to pray; and when it was evening, He was there alone. But the boat was already a long distance from the land, battered by the waves; for the wind was contrary. And in the fourth watch of the night, He came to them, walking on the sea."*

Matthew 14:28

> *"Peter said to Him, 'Lord, if it is You, command me to come to You on the water.'"*

Jeremiah 29:11

> *"'For I know the plans that I have for you,'*

declares the Lord, 'plans for welfare and not for calamity to give you a future and a hope.'"

CHAPTER 2- INSECURITIES

Genesis 1:26-28

"Then God said, 'Let Us make man in Our image, according to Our likeness; and let them rule over the fish of the sea and over the birds of the sky and over the cattle and over all the earth, and over every creeping thing that creeps on the earth.' God created man in His own image, in the image of God He created him; male and female He created them. God blessed them; and God said to them, 'Be fruitful and multiply, and fill the earth, and subdue it; and rule over the fish of the sea and over the birds of the sky and over every living thing that moves on the earth.'"

1 Samuel 9:21

"Saul replied, 'Am I not a Benjamite, of the smallest of the tribes of Israel, and my family the least of all the families of the tribe of Benjamin? Why then do you speak to me in this way?'"

Romans 12:4-5

"For just as we have many members in one

body and all the members do not have the same function, so we, who are many, are one body in Christ, and individually members one of another."

Habakkuk 2:2-3

"Then the Lord answered me and said, 'Record the vision and inscribe it on tablets, That the one who reads it may run. For the vision is yet for the appointed time; It hastens toward the goal and it will not fail. Though it tarries, wait for it; For it will certainly come, it will not delay.'"

1 Samuel 10:20-23

"Thus, Samuel brought all the tribes of Israel near, and the tribe of Benjamin was taken by lot. Then he brought the tribe of Benjamin nearby its families, and the Matrite family was taken. And Saul the son of Kish was taken; but when they looked for him, he could not be found. Therefore, they inquired further of the Lord, 'Has the man come here yet?' So, the Lord said, 'Behold, he is hiding himself by the baggage.' So, they ran and took him from there, and when he stood among the people, he was taller than any of the people from his shoulders upward."

1 Samuel 15:11-12

>*"'I regret that I have made Saul king, for he has turned back from following Me and has not carried out My commands.' And Samuel was distressed and cried out to the Lord all night. Samuel rose early in the morning to meet Saul; and it was told Samuel, saying, 'Saul came to Carmel, and behold, he set up a monument for himself, then turned and proceeded on down to Gilgal.'"*

Exodus 3:11-12

>*"But Moses said to God, 'Who am I, that I should go to Pharaoh, and that I should bring the sons of Israel out of Egypt?' And He said, 'Certainly I will be with you, and this shall be the sign to you that it is I who have sent you: when you have brought the people out of Egypt, you shall worship God at this mountain.'"*

Philippians 4:6-9

>*"Be anxious for nothing, but in everything by prayer and supplication with thanksgiving let your requests be made known to God. And the peace of God, which surpasses all comprehension, will guard your hearts and your minds in Christ Jesus. Finally, brethren, whatever is true, whatever is honorable,*

whatever is right, whatever is pure, whatever is lovely, whatever is of good repute, if there is any excellence and if anything, worthy of praise, dwell on these things. The things you have learned and received and heard and seen in me, practice these things, and the God of peace will be with you."

CHAPTER 3- THE SHEPHERD IN ME

Jeremiah 1:5

" 'Before I formed you in the womb I knew you, and before you were born, I consecrated you; I have appointed you a prophet to the nations.' "

1 Samuel 17:26

"Then David spoke to the men who were standing by him, saying, 'What will be done for the man who kills this Philistine and takes away the reproach from Israel? For who is this uncircumcised Philistine, that he should taunt the armies of the living God?' "

Matthew 14:13-21

"Now when Jesus heard about John, He withdrew from there in a boat to a secluded place by Himself; and when the people heard

of this, they followed Him on foot from the cities. When He went ashore, He saw a large crowd, and felt compassion for them and healed their sick. When it was evening, the disciples came to Him and said, " 'This place is desolate and the hour is already late; so, send the crowds away, that they may go into the villages and buy food for themselves.' But Jesus said to them, 'They do not need to go away; you give them something to eat!' They said to Him, 'We have here only five loaves and two fish.' And He said, 'Bring them here to Me.' Ordering the people to sit down on the grass, He took the five loaves and the two fish, and looking up toward heaven, He blessed the food, and breaking the loaves He gave them to the disciples, and the disciples gave them to the crowds, and they all ate and were satisfied. They picked up what was left over of the broken pieces, twelve full baskets. There were about five thousand men who ate, besides women and children."

CHAPTER 4- WORK

Genesis 2:2-3

"By the seventh day God completed His work which He had done, and He rested on the seventh day from all His work which He had done. Then God blessed the seventh day and

180

sanctified it, because in it He rested from all His work which God had created and made."

Genesis 6 - Whole chapter

Colossians 3:23-24

"Whatever you do, do your work heartily, as for the Lord rather than for men, knowing that from the Lord you will receive the reward of the inheritance. It is the Lord Christ whom you serve."

Matthew 20:28

"Just as the Son of Man did not come to be served, but to serve, and to give His life a ransom for many."

Genesis 2:7

"Then the Lord God formed man of dust from the ground, and breathed into his nostrils the breath of life; and man became a living being."

Mark 4:35-39

"On that day, when evening came, He said to them, 'Let us go over to the other side.' Leaving the crowd, they took Him along with them in the boat, just as He was; and other boats were with Him And there arose a fierce gale of wind, and the waves were breaking

over the boat so much that the boat was already filling up. Jesus Himself was in the stern, asleep on the cushion; and they woke Him and said to Him, 'Teacher, do You not care that we are perishing?' And He got up and rebuked the wind and said to the sea, 'Hush, be still.' And the wind died down and it became perfectly calm."

CHAPTER 5- LIKE A PALM TREE

Luke 14 - Whole Chapter

John 12 - Whole Chapter

Matthew 21 - Whole Chapter

Exodus 15:27

> *"Then they came to Elim where there were twelve springs of water and seventy date palms, and they camped there beside the waters."*

1 Thessalonians 5:11

> *"Therefore encourage one another and build up one another, just as you also are doing."*

Psalms 121:1-2

> *"I will lift up my eyes to the mountains; From where shall my help come? My help comes*

from the Lord, who made heaven and earth. "

Isaiah 41:10

"Do not fear, for I am with you; Do not anxiously look about you, for I am your God. I will strengthen you, surely, I will help you, Surely, I will uphold you with My righteous right hand."

CHAPTER 6: ANTICIPATIONS AND REACTIONS

Exodus 20:8-11

"Remember the sabbath day, to keep it holy. Six days you shall labor and do all your work, but the seventh day is a sabbath of the Lord your God; in it you shall not do any work, you or your son or your daughter, your male or your female servant or your cattle or your sojourner who stays with you. For in six days the Lord made the heavens and the earth, the sea and all that is in them, and rested on the seventh day; therefore, the Lord blessed the sabbath day and made it holy."

Hebrews 11:7

"By faith Noah, being warned by God about things not yet seen, in reverence prepared an ark for the salvation of his household,

by which he condemned the world, and became an heir of the righteousness which is according to faith."

Genesis 6-7 - Whole Chapters

Genesis 6:22

"Thus, Noah did; according to all that God had commanded him, so he did."

CHAPTER 7- WHY NOT ME

1 Corinthians 10:13

"No temptation has overtaken you but such as is common to man; and God is faithful, who will not allow you to be tempted beyond what you are able, but with the temptation will provide the way of escape also, so that you will be able to endure it."

Psalms 73:1-3

"Surely God is good to Israel, to those who are pure in heart! But as for me, my feet came close to stumbling, my steps had almost slipped. For I was envious of the arrogant As I saw the prosperity of the wicked."

Romans 12:9-10

"Let love be without hypocrisy. Abhor what is evil; cling to what is good. Be devoted to one another in brotherly love; give preference to one another in honor;"

CHAPTER 8- DO I HAVE IT ALL WRONG?

Proverbs 3:6 NLT

"Seek his will in all you do, and he will show you which path to take."

Matthew 6:32:33

"For the Gentiles eagerly seek all these things; for your heavenly Father knows that you need all these things. But seek first His kingdom and His righteousness, and all these things will be added to you."

James 2:26

"For just as the body without the spirit is dead, so also faith without works is dead."

Esther 4:14

" 'For if you remain silent at this time, relief and deliverance will arise for the Jews from another place and you and your father's house will perish. And who knows whether you have not attained royalty for such a time

as this?'"

Matthew 25:14-30

Parable of the Talents

Luke 9:23

"And He was saying to them all, 'If anyone wishes to come after Me, he must deny himself, and take up his cross daily and follow Me.'"

CHAPTER 9- A NEW NORMAL

Romans 11:29-31

"For the gifts and the calling of God are irrevocable. For just as you once were disobedient to God, but now have been shown mercy because of their disobedience, so these also now have been disobedient, that because of the mercy shown to you they also may now be shown mercy."

Matthew 6:14-15

"For if you forgive others for their transgressions, your heavenly Father will also forgive you. But if you do not forgive others, then your father will not forgive your transgressions."

Mark 11:24-25

"Therefore, I say to you, all things for which you pray and ask, believe that you have received them, and they will be granted you. Whenever you stand praying, forgive, if you have anything against anyone, so that your Father who is in heaven will also forgive you your transgressions."

Ephesians 4:31-32

"Let all bitterness and wrath and anger and clamor and slander be put away from you, along with all malice. Be kind to one another, tender-hearted, forgiving each other, just as God in Christ also has forgiven you."

Hebrews 8:12

"For I will be merciful to their iniquities, And I will remember their sins no more."

Luke 14:1-2

"It happened that when He went into the house of one of the leaders of the Pharisees on the Sabbath to eat bread, they were watching Him closely. And there in front of Him was a man suffering from dropsy. And Jesus answered and spoke to the lawyers and Pharisees, saying, 'Is it lawful to heal on the Sabbath, or not?' But they kept silent. And He took hold of him and healed him, and sent

him away."

Luke 17:12-19

> *"As He entered a village, ten leprous men who stood at a distance met Him; and they raised their voices, saying, 'Jesus, Master, have mercy on us!' When He saw them, He said to them, 'Go and show yourselves to the priests.' And as they were going, they were cleansed. Now one of them, when he saw that he had been healed, turned back, glorifying God with a loud voice, and he fell on his face at His feet, giving thanks to Him. And he was a Samaritan. Then Jesus answered and said, 'Were there not ten cleansed? But the nine—where are they? Was no one found who returned to give glory to God, except this foreigner?' And He said to him, 'Stand up and go; your faith has made you well.'"*

Proverbs 19:8

> *"He who gets wisdom loves his own soul; He who keeps understanding will find good."*

CHAPTER 10 - DISRUPT THE ROOM

Mark 16:15-16

> *"And He said to them, 'Go into all the world*

and preach the gospel to all creation. He who has believed and has been baptized shall be saved; but he who has disbelieved shall be condemned.'"

Hebrews 6:17-18

"In the same way God, desiring even more to show to the heirs of the promise the unchangeableness of His purpose, interposed with an oath, so that by two unchangeable things in which it is impossible for God to lie, we who have taken refuge would have strong encouragement to take hold of the hope set before us."

Exodus 6:17-18

"The sons of Gershon: Libni and Shimei, according to their families. The sons of Kohath: Amram and Izhar and Hebron and Uzziel; and the length of Kohath's life was one hundred and thirty-three years."

Exodus 1:15-22

"Then the king of Egypt spoke to the Hebrew midwives, one of whom was named Shiphrah and the other was named Puah; and he said, "When you are helping the Hebrew women to give birth and see them upon the birthstool, if it is a son, then you shall put him to death; but if it is a daughter, then she shall live.'

But the midwives feared God, and did not do as the king of Egypt had commanded them, but let the boys live. So, the king of Egypt called for the midwives and said to them, 'Why have you done this thing, and let the boys live?' The midwives said to Pharaoh, 'Because the Hebrew women are not as the Egyptian women; for they are vigorous and give birth before the midwife can get to them.' So, God was good to the midwives, and the people multiplied, and became very mighty. Because the midwives feared God, He established households for them. Then Pharaoh commanded all his people, saying, 'Every son who is born you are to cast into the Nile, and every daughter you are to keep alive.'"

Exodus 3:10-13

"'Therefore, come now, and I will send you to Pharaoh, so that you may bring My people, the sons of Israel, out of Egypt.' But Moses said to God, 'Who am I, that I should go to Pharaoh, and that I should bring the sons of Israel out of Egypt?' And He said, 'Certainly I will be with you, and this shall be the sign to you that it is I who have sent you: when you have brought the people out of Egypt, you shall worship God at this mountain.' Then Moses said to God, 'Behold, I am going

to the sons of Israel, and I will say to them, 'The God of your fathers has sent me to you.' Now they may say to me, 'What is His name?' What shall I say to them?'"

Exodus 6:1

"Then the Lord said to Moses, 'Now you shall see what I will do to Pharaoh; for under compulsion he will let them go, and under compulsion he will drive them out of his land.'"

Genesis 15:13-14

"God said to Abram, 'Know for certain that your descendants will be strangers in a land that is not theirs, where they will be enslaved and oppressed four hundred years. But I will also judge the nation whom they will serve, and afterward they will come out with many possessions.'"

John 2:3-6

"When the wine ran out, the mother of Jesus said to Him, 'They have no wine.' And Jesus said to her, 'Woman, what does that have to do with us? My hour has not yet come.' His mother said to the servants, 'Whatever He says to you, do it.' Now there were six stone waterpots set there for the Jewish custom of purification, containing twenty or thirty

gallons each."

John 2:8-10

"And He said to them, 'Draw some out now and take it to the headwaiter.' So, they took it to him. When the headwaiter tasted the water which had become wine, and did not know where it came from (but the servants who had drawn the water knew), the headwaiter called the bridegroom, and said to him, 'Every man serves the good wine first, and when the people have drunk freely, then he serves the poorer wine; but you have kept the good wine until now.'"

Luke 5:17-25

"One day He was teaching; and there were some Pharisees and teachers of the law sitting there, who had come from every village of Galilee and Judea and from Jerusalem; and the power of the Lord was present for Him to perform healing. And some men were carrying on a bed a man who was paralyzed; and they were trying to bring him in and to set him down in front of Him. But not finding any way to bring him in because of the crowd, they went up on the roof and let him down through the tiles with his stretcher, into the middle of the crowd, in front of Jesus. Seeing their faith, He said, 'Friend, your sins are forgiven

you.' The scribes and the Pharisees began to reason, saying, 'Who is this man who speaks blasphemies? Who can forgive sins, but God alone?' But Jesus, aware of their reasonings, answered and said to them, 'Why are you reasoning in your hearts? Which is easier, to say, "Your sins have been forgiven you," or to say, "Get up and walk?" But so that you may know that the Son of Man has authority on earth to forgive sins,'—He said to the paralytic— 'I say to you, get up, and pick up your stretcher and go home.' Immediately he got up before them, and picked up what he had been lying on, and went home glorifying God."

Matthew 21:12-14

"And Jesus entered the temple and drove out all those who were buying and selling in the temple, and overturned the tables of the money changers and the seats of those who were selling doves. And He said to them, 'It is written, "My house shall be called a house of prayer"; but you are making it a robbers' den.' And the blind and the lame came to Him in the temple, and He healed them."

Acts 2:2-4

"And suddenly there came from heaven a noise like a violent rushing wind, and it filled

*the whole house where they were sitting.
And there appeared to them tongues as of
fire distributing themselves, and they rested
on each one of them. And they were all filled
with the Holy Spirit and began to speak with
other tongues, as the Spirit was giving them
utterance."*

Revelation 1:8

*" 'I am the Alpha and the Omega,' says the
Lord God, 'who is and who was and who is
to come, the Almighty.'"*